THE COAL-SCUTTLE BRIGADE

The Coal-Scuttle Brigade

Alexander McKee

NEW ENGLISH LIBRARY
TIMES MIRROR

First published in 1957 by Souvenir Press Ltd. in Great Britain.
© by Alexander McKee 1957

*

THIS SPECIALLY ABRIDGED NEL PAPERBACK EDITION JANUARY 1973
Reprinted May 1973

*

NEL Books are published by
New English Library Limited from Barnard's Inn, Holborn, London, E.C.1.
Made and printed in Great Britain by Hunt Barnard Printing Ltd., Aylesbury, Bucks.

45001354 5

Contents

Foreword

The strange thing about this story is that some of the fiercest convoy battles of the war could take place literally on England's doorstep – a few miles off shore – and yet remain almost unknown except to those intimately concerned, who took it anyway for granted. I didn't – and this book is the result.

The accounts thus far published are meagre in the extreme, rarely more than a paragraph or two in books or magazines devoted to some other subject. The survivors possess a few action reports, diaries, photographs and faded newspaper cuttings; but the bulk of the story remained locked in the memories of those who took part and to whom I am indebted for the courtesy and eagerness with which they helped my investigations. In many ways it was like a detective investigation for, though events were well remembered, dates were often lost.

In particular, I should like to mention the help given me by Captain J. H. Potts, M.B.E., Captain C. L. Sclanders, M.B.E., and Captain F. Hadlow – all collier Masters – and J. R. Gallagher, B.E.M., formerly a Merchant Navy gunner. For the Navy and Army contribution to the convoys, both on board the merchantmen and in the escorts. I am indebted to Captain R. K. Spencer, V.R.D., R.N.V.R., Lieutenant-Colonel H. P. Stephenson, O.B.E., Commander F. C. Broderick, R.N. (Retd), Lieutenant-Commander A. J. G. Matthews, D.S.C., M.M., R.N.V.R., Lieutenant-Commander A. M. Kinnersley Saul, R.D., R.N.R., Mr W. C. Parncutt, Mr G. Glover, and Mr F. Duke. For research into events at the coal wharves I must thank Mr G. R. Baynton, of Dover; Mr T. J. Hay and Mr A. Duke, of Portsmonth; Mr S. W. Dennett, Chairman of the Phoenix Coal Co. Ltd, Mr G. I. F. Thomas, Mr A. Reid, and Mr W. Downie – all of Southampton; and many others, too numerous to mention.

I wish also to thank the Department of the Chief of Naval Information, the Admiralty Record Office, and the Queen's Harbour Master's department at Portsmouth for their co-operation in supplying many details not to be found in the brief outline given by the official history. This has enabled me to check dates, facts and figures which witnesses warned me were only approximate, as they were given from memory as much as seventeen years after the events.

It was, to me, surprising that these recollections proved extremely accurate, erring if at all on the side of underestimation. It seems that the most striking incidents have been, so to speak, embalmed by constant repetition and so preserved, much as folk tales are, at least during the lifetime of those who took part. Though much of the detail may have been forgotten, this book will have served its purpose if it preserves, at least in part, what is in many respects an epic story of the sea.

For the confused actions – the various running fights – I have tried to find more than one witness and have usually succeeded in obtaining the testimony of half a dozen; but for any errors of fact or transcription there may be, and for all opinions expressed, I must take sole responsibility.

ALEXANDER McKEE.

Rowlands Castle,
September, 1957.

1 · Black Thursday

DURING the summer of 1940, the sea route between Southend and Southampton became the most bitterly contested stretch of water in the world. By no coincidence whatever, it was also the area selected by the German Army for their landings, with the line Thames Estuary–Portsmouth listed as 'Operational Objective No. 1'.* The first essential for the crossing was to establish absolute and unquestioned dominance of the Channel in that area. By aircraft and guns, it was to be swept clear for the invasion armadas carrying the German 9th and 16th Armies to the assault.

It was the traditional crossing point of armies into England. Two Caesars had taken this route; so had William the Norman with his armoured horsemen and pre-fabricated castles carried in his assault craft; the Spaniards had intended it, and so had the French. Now, once more, one of the world's decisive battles was to be fought here. And into the battle, through the heart of the waters which must be made German if Hitler was to land in England, sailed – not warships bristling for battle – but grimy little colliers, carrying coal and coke for the factories and homes of southern England.

The designation of the collier convoy that passed the Straits of Dover on 25th July was C.W.8. That is, number eight collier convoy bound to the west. Convoys travelling to the east were designated C.E. There were, to start with, twenty-one merchant ships – small, and stained with the dirt of many years service in a grimy trade. They looked hardly worth defending. The armament of many of them consisted of a single Lewis gun. As they came out of the Thames from Southend, their lookouts saw a single 'snooper' plane keeping watch from seaward. Messages would be passing back now to the dive-bombers on their forward aerodromes behind Calais.

The convoy kept steadily on down the coast of Kent, to the slow beat of their engines. And some of those ships were very slow.

* Army Group Order No. 1 for the conduct of Operation SEALION.

They rounded the North Foreland in two divisions and turned down towards the Channel. The 'snooper' plane turned away – its job done. At four in the afternoon, with the convoy fairly in the Straits, John Gallagher, merchant navy gunner in the collier *Tamworth*, saw a horde of specks flying over the French coast – flying parallel to the coast, westward with the convoy, and climbing. They were getting height into the sun. He turned to the Second Mate, and reported: 'Enoch, there's a swarm of bees away to port.' The Second Mate answered, derisively: 'You've got specks in front of your eyes'.

Gallagher pondered a crushing reply, but before he had the words sorted out it was clear enough that the bees were of the stinging kind. The klaxon horn alarm for 'action stations' blared through the ship, and out across the water to their mates in convoy. Astern of them, the collier *Leo* of Hull was already closed up. They waved to the gunners of the *Leo*. And the men of the *Leo* waved back.

What happened next was very fast, very confusing; and spread out over many miles of sea and sky. No one saw it all, and no one afterwards could quite remember the exact sequence of events. There was the tearing howl of the dive-bombers plummeting down out of the sun, peeling off from their formation one after another, like divers from a board. There was a lot of smoke on the water. There were solid walls of spray bursting up from the Channel. A motor craft came out of the spray and smoke, and it didn't look like one of ours. It looked like an E-boat. The *Tamworth's* stern 12-pdr trained round and fired, and the motor-boat went back into the smoke.

Gallagher looked over to where a Dutch 'scuffler' had been keeping station in the convoy, and saw men rowing; he wondered what fishermen were doing, so far out in the Channel; and said so. Someone replied: 'It's the "scuffler". They've abandoned ship. She's gone.'

Four Junkers 87s came rocketting over the waves towards the *Tamworth*, coming in on the starboard quarter, machine-guns going – and hitting. Apparently attacking, they were making a low-level get-away, and covering their flight with machine-gun fire, to discourage the British gunners. But, though the stern 12-pdr wouldn't bear, Eric Speakman on the bridge, hemmed into his concrete emplacement behind twin Lewis guns, was grinning his head off as he blazed away. Then the planes were over them, and gone; vanished with that lightning speed whch so astonished men unused to it.

And astern the scene looked different. There was no *Leo* of Hull steadily shouldering the waves behind them. Instead, there was the bottom of a ship rolling in the water, with two men standing on the propeller shaft, and the upturned hull drifting slowly astern of the convoy.

The *Tamworth* stopped at that moment, as though she had hit a cliff. She rose, in a great wall of water, out of the water; and then fell back, to lie silent and wallowing in the Channel, engines stopped, and out of control. A stick of bombs had burst in the water, underneath her keel. And down came the next flock of dive-bombers.

There were bombers falling on them from above; and bombers pulling out of their dives, slow and vulnerable for a few fleeting moments, as the pilots pulled up the dive-brakes. There was no question of picking a target, but simply of taking them as they came. Gallagher saw the next one – he even saw the head of the pilot – and it meant nothing to him at all. There was neither emotion nor calculation – no time for theory of gunnery, for estimating the amount of deflection to give, for aiming off. Useless to fire at an aircraft, for you only hit where it has been; you have to fire in front – at where it will be when your projectiles get there. But there was no time for brain-work now; it was the time for instinctive firing, like a shot-gun swung from the shoulder at a flock of partridges. And Gallagher fired.

But it was not a shot-gun – it was a 12-pdr. There was a stunning noise in his ears, and then he was being kicked and slapped, and there were voices yelling in his ear. Above the ship, a few hundred yards up, was a cloud of smoke and fragments. Dazed with noise, and a slight wound, Gallagher couldn't make out what had happened. In fact, the men around him were shouting: 'You got it, you got it, you got it!' – and jumping with glee. The Junkers 87 had blown up; probably the petrol tanks had exploded.

There was a shout from the bridge: 'Stand by to abandon ship!' The collier's deck, just forward of the bridge, was buckled and humped up; the bulwarks were twisted; the engine-room ladders wrecked, and the main engines damaged, with steam escaping.

Between them and the French coast was an ever-lengthening wall of smoke – a 'B'-class destroyer was laying the screen for the *Tamworth* and the other lame ducks that lay stopped on the water. One small ship was crawling away to beach herself; a bomb, bursting in her cargo of cement, had covered her with it.

11

Astern, the *Leo* had gone. They heard later that her crew had twice abandoned ship, after being hit; but the first time, remembering that their 'number ones' were still on board, they had gone back for them; then rowed away for the last time, as their ship turned turtle. The ship directly ahead of the *Tamworth* had gone, too, and the *Tamworth* herself was crippled in the water, waiting for a tug to come out from Dover; and as she waited, more dive-bombers came out from France; and as they attacked, from all the British ships, cripples included, came the answering stab and rattle of gunfire.

The watchers at Dover – the cliffs were black with them, and the rooftops and top windows of buildings – watched the battle breathlessly. Half the world's press was there, and they have recorded how ashamed and futile it felt, merely to be a spectator of life-and-death in that vast natural arena under Dover cliffs.

One ship was beached under Shakespeare Cliff; then the *Tamworth* came in, wallowing behind a tug.

Dover Harbour is formed by two long breakwaters, reaching out in an arc; the *Tamworth* was towed to the coal wharf on the western arm. Two other vessels crippled in the attack were towed here; first a British ship, very low in the water, which – just as she was secured by the mooring lines fore and aft – lurched, and sank to the bottom; and besides her, a damaged Norwegian which lasted only a little longer. Moored to seaward of the *Tamworth*, she was hit a few minutes later in another bombing attack, pressed home under Dover cliffs; and sank.

It was now about 4.30 p.m. Two British destroyers were leaving harbour; and they were going out like speedboats, the white wash piling up under their sterns. The convoy was still in sight – away towards Folkestone. It no longer steamed in two long, proud lines, for nearly half the ships were gone. And now the Germans were making a last, determined effort to destroy it utterly; this time their attack was on the surface. The message that had reached the destroyers was: 'E-boats coming out of Calais: go and clobber them.' Or words to that effect.

This Destroyer Flotilla was based on Dover as an anti-invasion striking force, and to give distant cover to the convoys. Its role was offensive: to patrol Calais and Boulogne at night and, if the invasion armadas came out, catch them with their pants down, on their own doorstep. The crews had no doubt they could do it. In case of some assault craft getting through in foggy weather, an auxiliary Patrol of miscellaneous yachts and motor-boats patrolled on our side, close in shore. The destroyers habitually operated on the other side; but not in daylight, for their anti-aircraft armament was weak. The single pompom of one of the destroyers now going out habitually jammed every fifth round – a sharp blow on the breech with a mallet bringing it to its senses – so it fired in distinctive rhythm pom-pom-pom-pom-pom – bonk! – pom-pom-pom-pom-pom – bonk!

From the rooftops of Dover, through field glasses, the enemy was already in sight – dark specks crawling across the sea, outwards from the French coast. They only appeared to crawl; actually, they were racing over the surface at 40 knots, almost invisible behind their bow waves, their engines growling and snarling at top revolutions, the sea wildly disturbed behind them. Their pendants snapped in the wind and their torpedo tubes, like metal eyes, pointed at the battered merchantmen. Not only the world's press was watching, but the womenfolk of Dover – housewives left the sink and chambermaids dropped their brooms, to run to the windows and watch in fascinated horror the conflict of the gladiators.

The British did not send the whole flotilla – the enemy was not big enough for that – they sent *Brilliant* and *Boreas*. Within a minute of the message being received, they had slipped their buoys, gone curving out of harbour, and stepped on everything. At 35 knots they went slap for the E-boats, their sterns sunk low in the water and the stern-waves streaming higher than the deck. If the E-boats could get among the colliers it would be rather like a professional pug slamming an innocent bystander; but they couldn't. The destroyers got there first and at 5 o'clock, with impact fuses, they opened fire. The range was two miles.

The white water-spouts crept lazily up among the racing E-boats, and the splinters shrieked overhead. The Germans drove on through the fire; then there was an abrupt change in silhouette – they were turning; and as they turned, they made smoke. It rolled in drifting clouds across the water, and in it burst the destroyers' shells, and now and again could be seen the bobbing hull of an E-boat, tearing along. And then the silhouettes changed again – they were showing their sterns; they were going back to France. Wisely, for a destroyer is the E-boat's deadliest opponent. And now it was the turn of the destroyers to face unequal odds.

As the damaged E-boats retired, German guns on Cap Gris-Nez opened fire on the two destroyers. It was small-calibre shell-fire, for the heavy cross-Channel guns were not yet in position, and it was ineffective. Lieutenant-Commander Broderick, the senior of the two destroyer captains, was then told to return to Dover.

The *Brilliant* and the *Boreas* turned for home, their thin hulls trembling with the drive of their 34,000 horsepower engines. They were out in mid-Channel, far from the protection of the Dover guns and the British fighters. There was a swarm of specks coming out from the French coast, rapidly overtaking them. About two dozen Junkers 87s, stepped up in echelon, ready to peel off for the dive from 10,000 feet.

Standing by the chart-table on the bridge of the *Brilliant* were the Navigator and the Yeoman of Signals, William Parncutt. They saw the first stuka press its attack to the last possible moment – right down to mast-height – they saw the bomb leave the aircraft's belly and come straight at them. It seemed bigger than the ship, expanding all the time in the few seconds of its fall. That was the impression it gave; and few people could have been so close to a falling 1,100-lb. bomb and survived to describe the sensation. They both put their heads under the chart table.

But the deck was already heeling over, the ship seeming to spin round almost in its own length, for the captain – Lieutenant-Commander Broderick – had judged his moment with razor-edged accuracy. With just enough time to avoid the bomb, but with insufficient for the German pilot to alter his aim, he had given: 'Hard-a-starboard.'

The watchers on the cliff saw the sea open in a solid-seeming spurt of spray and smoke, hundreds of feet high, the rapidly-turning destroyer momentarily lost to view. A deluge of water swept the chart room, soaking Parncutt and the Navigator to the waist; then the *Brilliant* was racing on, engines still thundering at top revolutions, her guns hammering away at the successive plunges of dive-bomber after dive-bomber.

After the stukas came a shallow-diving swarm of Dornier 17s; and time after time the watchers on the cliffs saw vast walls of water go up, blotting out the ships; and always, out of the falling water and drifting smoke, when it seemed they must have gone, the knife-bows of the *Brilliant* and the *Boreas*. It was off-putting for the pilots. But they were as professional as their opponents. They put two bombs through the stern of the *Brilliant*, which didn't explode and went right through; and they got a direct hit on the bridge of the *Boreas*, killing or wounding about thirty-five men. And they kept on attacking, right up to the moment of entering harbour, with stukas once again.

While this last attack was still in progress, the destroyers received a signal that fighter cover was now overhead; but, in fact, it was nowhere near, the fighters having flown far out to the French coast. When the damage was examined in harbour it was found that the two bombs which had struck the quarter deck of the *Brilliant* had both of them missed the propeller shaft by about a foot, but the only real damage they had done was to flood the Tiller Flat. On the other hand, there was a lot of damage by the near-misses, which had punched the water against the side of the ship; the cast-iron supports of the Boiler Room fans were cracked, purely by concussion. The heavy casualties in the *Boreas* had been caused by the bombs passing through the bridge and exploding below in the Galley Flat.

Only eleven ships of the convoy passed Dungeness; next day, three more of them were sunk. Convoy C.W.8 had endured, as Captain Sclanders of the *Tamworth* put it, 'a heavy dusting off Dover'. The town itself was full of 'bombed-out' seamen. In soaked clothes, or in borrowed ones, they sat about. At the moment of landing, and for several hours afterwards, many were in bad shape – trembling and taking cover at any air raid warning. But when the effects of shock and excitement wore off, most returned to normal; many, that night, were in the pubs, singing in chorus and showing no outward trace of their ordeal.

But they were civilians – they signed on for the voyage only; there was no power to make them sign on again; they could leave the sea altogether if they liked. How many would volunteer for a repeat dose? A good many did – and virtually all the officers.

Two days later, on 27th July, a destroyer was sunk off Dover. The German attacks were coming in mounting rhythm and the pace was becoming hot, even though only a small proportion of the Luftwaffe was as yet engaged. Dover, as an advanced base for the anti-invasion flotilla of destroyers, was abandoned. Apart from a few small minesweepers and tugs, nothing British moved in the Straits by day. The Germans had virtual control of the Channel at its narrowest point.

2 · Action This Day

*'Could you let me know on one sheet of paper what arrange-
ments you are making about the Channel convoys now that
the Germans are all along the French coast? The attacks on
the convoys yesterday, both from the air and by E-boats, were
very serious, and I should like to be assured this morning that
the situation is in hand and that the Air is contributing effec-
tively.'* (*Memo from Prime Minister, d/d 5th July, 1940.*)

'THE COAL-SCUTTLE BRIGADE' came into being, if not with a
bang, then at least with a rocket – in the shape of the above
memorandum, marked for 'Action This Day', from Winston
Churchill to the Vice-Chief of Naval Staff. It referred to the
mauling of a Channel convoy on the previous day – 4th July.

The mauling of the convoy produced the 'rocket'. The 'rocket'
produced action that very day. The Admiralty decided to stop all
normal Channel traffic – which included large ocean-going ships –
and to allow through the Channel only convoys of small coasting
vessels, mainly colliers. That is, the seaborne coal trade continued
– but London and Southampton, as major ports for convoys from
the west, were voluntarily put out of action. London still took a
proportion of its former traffic, for the East Coast route was less
closely threatened at that time. Down that route, in the first place,
sailed the colliers from the coal ports of the North. But the ports
of the south coast, great and small, were deserted. Only the
colliers and a few warships moved on that route.

After twenty days of air attack, even the colliers stopped. But
the halt was short-lived. Within a few weeks of 'Black Thursday',
the collier convoys had been re-started, with rapidly improvised
protection. They never stopped after that. But they had the
Channel to themselves. And, broadly speaking, that continued
until well into 1943, when the tide began to turn. Then, very
curious shipping movements began to take place in the Channel,
culminating in a very different sort of Channel convoy. And in
the end, before the war ended, the 'Coal-Scuttle Brigade' went to
France

Along the coast-line of Occupied Europe, the Germans, too, ran their coastal convoys. At first, as we did, in daylight; later, as we did, at night. And as they attacked our convoys, we attacked theirs. The end of 1942 marks approximately the turning point: before that time, they had done our convoys serious damage and we had done little damage to theirs; after that time, they did us little hurt, and we started to hurt them. In other words, the battle of the coastal shipping routes followed the general pattern of the war. And this was because all the vital decisions affecting the events of 1940 had been taken by 1936. Men who died in 1940 did so as a result of something done – or not done – four years before. By no possible chance whatever could a major decision made in 1940 take effect until 1943. Bombers don't grow on trees. Tanks are not picked up, wild, in the hedgerows. And destroyers can't be forced, under glass, in two weeks. In 1940, many merchant sailors must have wished to God they could.

On 25th June there was a rush for the evening papers. The headlines read: 'Bugles Sounded "Cease Fire" in France This Morning.' In smaller type: 'At 12.35 this morning the Battle of France ended and the Battle of Britain began.'

Across the Dover Straits, the Germans had been three weeks in occupation. Gun emplacements were being built, and the guns lifted into position, particularly on the great headland of Cap Gris-Nez, 22 miles from Dover. Daily, German radio sets shook as the stations boomed out the swelling, confident march– Wir fahren gegen England. It thundered across the Channel to British listeners – about a third of them listened to Haw Haw and the German radio.

The guns were intended to cover with fire the flanks of the German invasion flotillas heading for the Dover area; and to keep their flanks guarded for the endless lines of supply ships that must sustain them. They were heavy guns, and there were many of them; even so, almost certainly not enough for the job they were supposed to do. In the event, they did not have to do it. The only targets that passed their muzzles were small warships and the slowly-lumbering colliers of the Channel convoys. In six weeks they would be ready to open fire.

The Luftwaffe had just completed an exhausting campaign. It had now to launch another – against England. The British fighter and bomber bases were long-prepared. The Germans' were not. They moved, where they could, into French aerodromes. There were not enough of them: more had to be built. Stores, workshops, transport, equipment of all kinds had to be moved from Germany to the Channel coast. The Luftwaffe was not ready yet, and the Battle of Britain had not begun. The whole force of the Luftwaffe was to be gathered together and flung in one overwhelming mass against the British Isles – the defence was to be steam-rollered. That great operation was given the code-name of Adlerangriff – Eagle Attack – and the day was planned for the first week of August. In fact, 'Eagle Day' did not come until 12th August – when it went off at half-cock – and on that day the actual Battle of Britain begins. What went before was the preliminary sparring match – and that was the Battle of the Channel Convoys.

The first aircraft to be flown into the French aerodromes on the Channel coast were fighters and light dive-bombers. They could operate from small airfields, and they did not need runways. They were designed for just such conditions as these. It was this force – a comparatively small one – which opened the batting.

The first phase lasted little more than a week – from 1st to 9th July. In those nine days the naval ports of Dover, Weymouth, Portland, Plymouth and Falmouth were bombed in daylight and there were seven attacks on convoys in the Channel. Among them, on 4th July, the ill-fated OA 178.

OA 178 passed Dover, westbound, on 3rd July. The German guns were not ready to fire, though field-grey working parties were struggling feverishly to get them into position. The convoy moved on slowly to the west. There were ships of all types and sizes in it – not just small coastal colliers. At lunch-time on the 4th it was off Portland. And there the Germans caught it. Handfuls of bombers – six at a time – protected by equally small groups of fighters, ripped down at it, almost without opposition from the R.A.F. They sent four ships to the bottom, and left nine damaged – stopped, burning, out of control. The remaining ships, as they steamed slowly to the west, left behind them a trail of wounded merchantmen and all the pitiful wreckage of war at sea – riddled lifeboats and men swimming in the oil-soaked sea.

Darkness had barely hidden their wounds before the next wave of attackers came in – E-boats this time. Only a handful of them – once again – but they sank one ship and damaged two more. This could hardly be blamed on the lack of fighters, but there was a howl of rage from the Navy. There were bitter accusations: 'No fighters and no escort worth talking about . . .

18

nobody to appeal to if the Air don't turn up . . . a criminally inefficient system.'*

OA 178 had sailed straight into inter-Service controversy of long-standing and great bitterness. It threatened to wreck Dowding's plans for the Battle of Britain, still to come. In some form or other, all countries possessing air forces as well as armies and navies, experienced it. It was inevitable, for their functions interlocked.

The Channel convoys were a catspaw in the deadly game just beginning. For the High Command of the Luftwaffe they were gambit No. 2 – in the game that was to end with the invasion of England, if the English reacted. Gambit No. 1 had been 'free chase' over England for the German fighters. But the English wouldn't fight. They would attack their coastal shipping – cut their trade routes – and force Fighter Command to battle in defence of them.

As long as only fighters came over, Fighter Command wouldn't play. Dowding had not the least intention of obliging the Luftwaffe. The Germans then played their second card – the 250 stukas available on the forward aerodromes in France. From the first week of July onwards they threw them at Channel convoys. They forced the R.A.F. to put up a token defence and notwithstanding that defence, drove all merchant ships out of the Channel. All except the colliers.

The south coast was dependent on sea-borne coal. 40,000 tons was needed per week. The colliers had to go through. And the Germans had to attack them, in order to bring the R.A.F. to battle. The Coal-Scuttle Brigade were launched upon their odyssey.

I make no apology for now dealing with the air situation. The colliers were bombed, not because they were colliers; not because the German thought them particularly valuable or important; they were attacked and sunk as a tactical move in the air battle between Fighter Command and the Luftwaffe. And that air battle was a preliminary to the Battle of Britain, which was in turn a preliminary to Operation SEALION – the invasion of England. The coastal convoys lost, during this opening phase, one ship sunk or damaged beyond repair out of every three that sailed.

Three great Air Fleets were moving into position in a great arc round the British Isles. Luftflotte 5 (Stumpff) was to operate against the East Coast from bases in Norway – this was the

* *Max Horton and the Western Approaches*, p. 91.

weakest of the three. Luftflotte 2 (Kesselring) was based in the Low Countries and Northern France – and it was this air fleet which had the duty of closing the Straits of Dover. Luftflotte 3 (Sperrle) was on its left – to the westward.

The Germans, too, had their inter-Service squabbles. An indication of how they had solved it lay in the fact that Kesselring – the man most concerned with attacks on Channel convoys – was not an airman at all. He was a soldier – and a soldier's soldier. It was Kesselring who afterwards declared that he couldn't get the R.A.F. to fight. Nor could he. His opponent, 'Stuffy' Dowding, had not the least intention of falling in with his enemy's moves – of letting the Luftwaffe dictate where, when, and under what conditions the battle should be fought.

In the quality of his aircraft, he had no advantage. Generally speaking, the Luftwaffe had better aircraft than the R.A.F. Dowding's actions, and the course of the battle, cannot be understood unless this fact is grasped. It is difficult to grasp, because of the weight of propaganda poured out then, and since. The official histories have corrected this – but they are not widely read. The only clue at the time was the consistently false note which was struck by the aeronautical press. They praised one German aircraft only – the Me 110. The Germans considered it a wretched flop. Two German aircraft they consistently and viciously denigrated – the Me 109 and the Ju 88. These two were better than anything we had.

They were better in performance, and they were better in detail design. The Germans had direct-injection engines, self-sealing fuel tanks, and rubber dinghies in their fighters – all of which the R.A.F. lacked. And the Me 109 was the fastest fighter in the world. Contemporary claims, officially made for the Spitfire at the time, are false. It was slower than the Me 109; and the Hurricane was slower still; and the two-seater Defiant, much-boosted, was a flying coffin. But the Spitfire was superior to the Me 109 in one respect – it was more manoeuvrable.

As far as battles over the Channel were concerned, the Luftwaffe had the advantage in quality of aircraft. The quality of the air crews is more difficult to compare; there was probably not much in it, but Fighter Command, for reasons mentioned later, may have had some ascendancy of morale.* As far as quantity was concerned, the Germans had a considerable overall advan-

* For full discussion of this subject, by fighter pilots on both sides, see: Pierre Clostermann, *The Big Show*, p. 166; and Adolf Galland, *The First and the Last*, p. 76.

tage – though not as great as was believed at the time; but it is vital to remember that the gap closed steadily during the period of attacks on convoys, owing to Dowding's policy. The result of their sufferings was not only to keep industry going in the south, but to double the number of fighters available for the Battle of Britain.

The force being built up for that battle was to be in a 'state of readiness' by 20th July. On that date the three air fleets facing England had, serviceable, some 800 bombers, 250 short-range dive-bombers, and 820 fighters.

On 6th September, with the Battle of Britain more than half over, the leading aeronautical journal in England (by then, virtually an official publication) announced that Germany possessed 7,000 bombers and 4,000 fighters, two-thirds of which were available for use against this country. The Luftwaffe records for the following day, 7th September, have been preserved. They are counter-signed by Albert Speer, and show that the number of German fighters serviceable and available for operations against England on that day was – 762. That is, about the same as Fighter Command.

Three months before, Fighter Command had had only about half that number of fighters. It was a surprising and quite decisive change. Dowding had known his advantage, and held it. The real, battle-winning superiority which the R.A.F. had over the Luftwaffe lay in the unique system of ground control – of warning and direction of fighters onto the enemy. Warned by radar and directed by R/T, the British fighters were under the thumb of their commander second by second. Whereas the Germans received orders in the briefing room before they left; and no more after that. They were fighting blind, against a foe who had most unexpectedly grown eyes where no eyes should be. It was the only system of its kind in the world, and when the German pilots realized what they were up against, they were dismayed.

But the system did not work very well over the Channel – the period between the radar warning and the arrival of the raiders was too short. It had never been designed to deal with this proposition. When planned, many years before the war, the assumption was that the bombers would be coming from Germany – not from the French coast. Literally, minutes counted now. A raid on targets inland, perhaps only five or ten minutes' flying time inland, made all the difference. And there, too, the raiders could be counted by the Observer Corps. For the early radar, though it gave accurately the bearing of the attackers, was often at fault in registering their numbers.

What happened over the Channel, only too often, was that a single German aircraft was reported flying in; and perhaps two fighters directed on to it. When they made their interception, they might find – not one lonely German – but a squadron. They were often outnumbered, and their casualties were high.

So, when the convoy-attack phase opened on 1st July, the defence was gravely handicapped. Warning would be received late, often too late to mass an equal number of British aircraft; the number of raiders might be larger than was indicated, sometimes very much larger; the British fighters were technically inferior to the German fighters, and especially so over the Channel and Channel coast; and the Germans, at that time, had a great overall superiority in numbers of fighters.

Fighter Command's lowest point was Dunkirk. On 4th June it had been reduced to 446 serviceable fighters – of which only 331 were Spitfires and Hurricanes. The others, though they might perhaps be of use, far inland, against unescorted bombers, had no chance against the Me 109s. For all practical purposes Fighter Command was outnumbered by nearly three to one in fighters; six to one in all.

It was vital that the new production coming from the factories, and the new pilots from the schools, should not be thrown in piece-meal; that the force should be conserved, and built up. By 11th August, the day before the Battle of Britain began, Dowding had nearly doubled his strength – he now had 704 fighters serviceable, of which no less than 620 were Spitfires and Hurricanes. It was just enough.

All this time, from the first serious attacks on Channel convoys in early July, Dowding was under intense pressure. He calculated that, for the full protection of shipping between Land's End and the Humber, he would need to employ 40 squadrons. If he did so, he would uncover the aircraft factories on which his Command depended for their reserves during the impending battle. All the fighters in the United Kingdom couldn't have protected both. Somebody had to get hurt. It was to be the convoys, and the men who sailed in them.

3 · The Battle of the Channel

SUCH was the background to that decisive battle, during which the coasters were to be sent on their death run. From 1st July, the German 'decoy ducks' – as the Messerschmitt pilots called the handful of Ju 87s they had to protect – were thrown at the Channel convoys as bait to bring the battered R.A.F. prematurely to battle.

One week later, the Channel lay deserted. The harbours, great and small, were stilled, the docks silent; ocean convoys bound for London were either diverted to west coast ports or went round Scotland to reach the Thames. Nothing moved, that summer, in the Channel except the essential coastal traffic – a few small colliers – some minesweepers, destroyers and patrol vessels.

Then at half past one on 10th July, with the sun high, 20 black bombers streamed out from Calais towards a convoy passing Dover. Six Hurricanes flew westward above the ships. They met the 40 fighters of the German escort – outnumbered nearly 7 to 1 by their own kind, 10 to 1 in all. No victory was won, or claimed, but they upset the attackers and one ship only was sunk.

On 11th July, the attack switched 200 miles to Lyme Bay, where ten Ju 87s went for an eastbound convoy, covered by 20 Me 109s. Three Hurricanes and six Spitfires engaged them, losing a third of their number in a few minutes, but again they upset the bombers and this time no ship was sunk. A few hours later, another attack came in. It was reported as a single German aircraft and six Hurricanes were sent to meet it. But the radar was unreliable in this respect – and what they met was a formation of more than fifty Germans. They got two of the Ju 87s and one ship only was damaged.

On 14th July another convoy was attacked in the Straits – photographs show the colliers *Betswood* and *Bovey Tracey*, and other ships not identifiable, vanishing in the thunderous uprush of smoke and water from the bombs. One coaster was towed into Dover with her stern blown off, two others and an escort destroyer were damaged. The Germans were beinning to get their eye in.

From that day onwards, the R.A.F. were under orders from

23

the War Cabinet to shoot down all German Red Cross planes hanging about near the convoys – and they sent a Heinkel 59 ambulance plane of the German Air-Sea Rescue service into the Channel off Walmer Castle. The Luftwaffe then sank the Folkestone Gate Lightship, in daylight, in clear view of Dover. The fighting spirit of both sides was not fanatical, merely stubborn. The Germans were determined to blast the British out of the Straits and sweep the Channel clear; the British had dug their toes in, and it was going to take a good deal to shift them. Inevitably, some of the crockery got broken.

As the destroyer *Brazen* went down in the Channel, there were wounded men, still at their posts, shooting back; and three bombers went into the Channel to join her on the bottom. On the 19th, there was a fiasco – a Defiant squadron brought down from Scotland to help the hard-pressed squadrons over the Straits was so badly mauled in its first action that it was sent straight back. The two-seater fighters – the British Defiant and the Me 110 – could now be discounted as inefficient and ineffectual. The pace was growing hot. On the 21st, came the turn of the Cherbourg squadrons – they struck at a convoy near the Isle of Wight, and all that day destroyers and tugs were going out of Portsmouth to rescue survivors and tow in disabled ships. And on the 25th, came 'Black Thursday' – the shattering in the Straits of convoy C.W.8.

Of the 21 colliers and coasters which sailed that day from Southend, only 11 passed Dungeness – and of these, only two reached their destination undamaged. So heavy and so continuous was the dive-bombing that no one knows how many attacks were made – the official history can say only, 'at least four'. And two days later, on the 27th, the Dover destroyers lost their Flotilla Leader, *H.M.S. Codrington*, and had *H.M.S. Walpole* damaged. Dover, as a base for anti-invasion destroyers, was abandoned. The 'flying artillery' of the Luftwaffe had virtually cleared the way across for their Army – in daylight.

A breathless silence settled down on the invasion coast. In front, the beaches were hedged with scaffolding, concrete blocks, barbed wire, and mines; behind, it was sealed off by checkpoints on the roads, through which no one was allowed to pass unless he lived on the coast. It was a genuine front-line feeling – of silence and desertion and barbed tension, broken suddenly by violent action, which stopped as suddenly as it began, leaving only the frightened screaming of the sea-gulls to die away gradually.

On the 29th, the Luftwaffe began, ominously, to push inland.

They struck now at Dover itself. But as the stukas began to pour down, the first Hurricanes were already turning in at 8,000 feet to the attack. The British pilots saw great fountains of spray explode in the harbour around the few ships left there, and they saw, stepped up in the sky, two more squadrons of stukas waiting their turn to dive. And then they were in among them. The Ju 87s were so slow that when pursued they seemed almost to come sliding backwards into the sights.

On 7th August, 25 merchant ships lay off Southend, cradled between the shores of Kent and Essex; all of them coasters, most of them colliers. They lay low in the water, heavy with grimy cargo from the coal ports of the north; their crews, for the most part, came from the same places as the cargoes – they were 'Geordies'.

There was tension among them now, that tight feeling at the back of the skull that you get when you know you're going into action – and they knew that now, for a certainty.

They were no longer serving their owners – the ships had been requisitioned by the Admiralty; they were no longer colliers trading to the south coast – they were part of a naval operation. They were going to force the Straits of Dover.

After they had settled down for a conference in the dance-hall on Southend pier, the Commodore had stood up. He wore the three stripes of a Commander, R.N.R., and he would be sailing in the leading ship of the port division. He looked like a man used to commanding ocean liners – 20,000 tons and 20 knots – and some of them had wondered what *he* was doing in a coasting job. The Captains of the two destroyers which would escort them were there, too.

Behind him, on a blackboard, was a diagram of the formation which the convoy would keep: they would be formed in two divisions, once they got outside the estuary; a destroyer would lead each division, keeping station slightly outside of it, so that a glance from her bridge would take in all the ships of that division; and for the same reason the larger ships would be at the head of the line, if possible. But some of the ships were not bound as far as the convoy dispersal point inside the Isle of Wight; they would leave the convoy and take their cargoes into ports which it passed on the way; and these ships would be on the tail end of the lines, to avoid having to turn and cross the course of the others in leaving.

From the diagram, they could see their own station in the

convoy; this, and their own destination, as well as other technical details were confirmed by a 'flimsy', copies of which had been handed round. They sat there, clutching them, as the Commodore rose to speak.

'Haw-Haw is saying that the Germans have closed the Channel. That it's no longer the English Channel – it's part of the German Ocean. We're here to prove him wrong.'

There was a shuffle of feet, and a bout of coughing.

'We don't give a damn for your coal.'

A quick muttering round the room, indignant and angry.

'We'd send you through empty, if we had to. It's a matter of prestige. Field Marshal Göring has told the world: "The Channel is in German hands". We're going to prove him wrong, even if we have to give you battleships to get you through; you'll run – *"light or lame"*.'

The room was dead quiet now. The Commodore went on to explain that what was intended was a combined naval and air operation to force a passage through the Straits. There would be a close escort, part of the way, of one trawler and two destroyers; other destroyers would be on call, at Portsmouth. No. 145 Squadron of Hurricanes would be standing by, at 'immediate readiness', during all the hours of daylight. But there would be very little daylight – they would be passing the Straits at night. They would be off Dover at midnight.

They would stop, on no account whatever; there would be rescue ships with them, to pick up survivors, and tugs to take charge of the cripples. And they would be surrounded by balloon ships.

In the afternoon of 7th August, convoy C.W.9 sailed from the Thames. They went out singly, because of the narrow channel, and took up convoy formation outside. It was noticeable, even at this early date, that they showed better discipline than the northbound convoys. There was a 'Gate' in the boom defences that stretched from the Isle of Grain to Shoeburyness, protecting the entrance to the Thames; and there was always a tendency for the independent-minded merchant ships to weigh anchor together, in a rush, and dash for it – like children tumbling out of school. No such disorder marked the 'Coal-Scuttle Brigade' and, as they gained experience, they got better and better, going out like rows of Guardsmen.

At two o'clock precisely, the signal flying from the Commodore's ship became executive; that is, it came fluttering down – meaning: 'Proceed'. And then, precisely, one after the other –

26

and not in a gaggle – the 'Coal-Scuttle Brigade' hauled up their anchors, and sailed for the 'Gate'. Once outside, they took up station in two divisions – that is, in two long parallel lines, with the Commodore flying his flag at the head of the port division and the Vice-Commodore flying his at the head of the starboard division. A naval operation was under weigh.

Off Sheerness, the escort came to join them, the destroyers rolling in the swell; from the Navy men closed up at their guns came a brief cheer for the lumbering colliers.

There were 25 ships in the convoy – each one with a different speed and a different turning circle; whenever they changed course, the inside ships had to slow, while the outside ships increased speed. Even keeping station on a straight course was difficult, at first, with so many types of ship and so many ships, and the inexperience of the masters in judging their exact distance from the vessel ahead. It was only a trick – done with a sextant; by measuring off the height of the next ahead, from waterline to masthead, and knowing in advance what that height was. But these were dour, independent, not very well educated men, masters of the instinctive tricks of their tricky coastal trade, and contemptuous of any unnecessary calculations that came out of a book.

Yet station keeping was vital, for if one ship was out of position, then every vessel behind her was also out of position. They mastered the art of it very soon.

All guns had been uncovered now; and individual gunners began to fire testing shots – tracer went streaking out over the water; it was blue and calm, with darker patches of green marking the cloud shadow. To starboard, the woods and fields of Kent sloped downwards to sandy beaches and the sea. To port, the empty sea heaved to the horizon: out there lay only the enemy. Then a helio began to wink from the senior escort vessel. They were approaching the North Foreland and would soon begin the long, slow turn to starboard that would take them into the Straits.

This was the danger point. The evidence was all around them: the sun, low on the horizon now, cast in dark silhouette the masts of many ships, sticking jaggedly out of the water; close inshore, where some unknown collier master had tried to beach his sinking ship, part of the bridge and hull of the wreck were above water, torn and jagged. Then it was night, and they were driving into the Straits.

Above them, the masts rolled across the night sky; beneath, the hammering engines urged them on; the Red Ensign on the stern fluttered in the wind, and the sound of bell buoys came tinkling across the sea. Surely the Germans knew they were coming. But there was no sign of alarm to seaward; and to starboard, the vague whiteness of the cliffs of Dover loomed comfortingly close. Every man who could, was on deck; and every man wore his lifejacket; the crews were still closed up around the guns; the master and his officers paced the narrow bridge, the Lewis gunner in one wing of it was directly under their eye. There would be no sleep for anyone this night.

Steadily, slowly, stretching for miles like a many-jointed monster, convoy C.W.9, with thumping engines, steamed on for the shelter of the Isle of Wight. It was midnight – and then it was the 8th of August. Men stared out to seaward – and saw many things which were not there; night plays tricks with the eyes, and with the nerves, but certainly the enemy was over there, and certainly he knew of their coming. His planes ranged over southern England all day: he must know. The night was full of eyes, watching the black waters.

At 3 o'clock, at the very darkest hour of the night, at the pit of man's vitality, when he has reached the nadir of the daily cycle and sleep should be at its deepest; at that moment, the quiet thumping rhythm of the gliding ships and the wash and suck of water was suddenly drowned by a violent noise from seaward. There was a blare and snarl of high-powered engines suddenly kicking into life; then an escort destroyer fired starshell, illuminating the sea in a ghastly greenish light. Instantly, the engine noise from seaward was cut off by the slam of gunfire: escort and convoy blazing away for all they were worth, the night sprinkled with red cascades of tracer.

It was an E-boat ambush. The Germans had known that they were coming known too the route they must use – the narrow channel swept every 24 hours by the minesweepers. They had crept up under cover of the darkness, engines throttled down; and then had waited there, rocking in the swell, engines dead, in ambush; waiting for the thump and thud of steamship engines in the night. When they started up, they were only a few hundred yards away.

It would be a cool man who could have remembered what happened next, in its proper sequence. Those who endured it – and survived – talk of 'a bit of a flap' – a confused impression of starshell-lit action and overwhelming noise; the ribbons of tracer and stabs of gunfire licking out from the hulls of the driving ships; of the streaming bow-waves of an E-boat, the splash of a torpedo loosed, and running; of ships zig-zagging to avoid torpedoes, and their engines battering away, shaking the hulls; of the dull boom – the white spray surging up the side – from a torpedo hit; of ships sinking and breaking up, of bits of ships sinking, and of ships colliding in their frantic efforts to avoid a torpedo; with men's voices crying in the darkness and drowned by the booming roar of the wasp-like E-boats screaming across the water at 35 knots.

William Dawson, master of the collier *John M*, steaming near the head of one line, saw Verey lights curving up from the darkness, port and starboard, from E-boats on either side of him trying to illuminate their prey; he heard a tremendous explosion astern, and saw the bow of a ship rise slowly out of the water as she began to slide slowly sternfirst under. A searchlight flashed on and swung – and there was an E-boat, near, clear and startled, 300 yards away from him on the starboard beam. The *John M's* Lewis gun began to hammer away at it – and the E-boat reacted like a startled horse; it heeled over in a turn of speed, with great arcs of spray sheeting from under the bows, and raced away into the darkness of the Channel.

One master gave 'Stand by anchors!' because he thought he was running up on the beach; he wasn't, he was merely steaming through hundreds of tons of floating coke from a sunken collier; the sea was covered with it.

Another collier master had seen the two ships ahead of him go up, and two others collide; then, suddenly, 'there was a lull in the flap'; the battle had either died down or moved away. Standing on the bridge, the Master and Mate, very wrought up, could hardly believe their luck to have survived this far.

At dawn the Master of the *John M* found himself alone, with only a few specks on the horizon: the convoy was scattered over ten miles of sea.

The *Holme Force* and the *Fife Coast* had gone to the bottom, with 30 or 40 foot holes torn in their hulls by the torpedoes; the *Polly M* had been hit, too, but she was still afloat, just. The *Ouse*, with helm hard over to avoid a torpedo racing at her, had collided with the *Rye*. She sank soon after, but the *Rye* was still afloat, damaged.

At half past eight that morning No. 145 Squadron 'scrambled' from Westhampnett, on receipt of the news that a convoy south of the Isle of Wight was being attacked by dive-bombers. The weather was not suitable for it, and hampered the Germans; then the Hurricanes arrived. They got in among the Junkers 87s and

29

broke up several of their formations, before themselves becoming mixed up with the escorting Me 109s. The scattered ships of C.W.9 could hear the battle going on, above and in the clouds – the growl of the engines and the stutter of machine-guns; and see some of it, machines racing through the gaps or ducking down under the cloud base and booming along in clear view; but what exactly was happening they had no idea. Bombs were certainly coming down, and the sea was exploding in fury; but it was all rather aimless. A black, gull-winged shape, descending with a metallic howling whine, struck the sea in a shower of spray, and vanished – that was a Junkers 87. Then all the noise began rapidly to move out to sea, and all was quiet. The Germans had gone; and no ships had been sunk.

At this point, officially, C.W.9 vanishes. C.W. convoys ran from Southend to Portsmouth, where most of the ships would disperse to the wharves at Southampton or Portsmouth itself. Those ships whose destination lay further west would form a new convoy, loosely described at the time as, simply, 'westbound', and might be joined by ships lying waiting for them in St Helen's Roads, near Ryde. Later, these convoys ran between Portsmouth and Plymouth, under no designation, for they were small; but the larger convoys between the British Channel ports and Plymouth were to be known as PW/WP convoys. In other words, the convoys from Southend served mainly south-eastern England; the convoys from the Bristol Channel served mainly south-western England; and the exceptions which proved the rule ran a shuttle service between the two.

So what was happening during the late morning and early afternoon of 8th August, was that some of the ships which had travelled in C.W.9 were heading westwards, south of the Isle of Wight, and being joined by ships which had lain waiting for their arrival in St Helen's Roads. Other ships which had been part of C.W.9 were making their way across Spithead into Portsmouth, for the coal wharves of the Camber and Rudmore, while others were going up the Solent to discharge at Southampton. But, since C.W.9 had been scattered and broken up by the E-boat attack, and never completely recovered, these movements were a good deal looser and less well-phased than they might have been. And at these movements, in much better weather, for the skies had now cleared, and with much greater numbers, for they knew that only numbers could annihilate – the Germans struck. It was a confused battle; many of the ships were caught, on their own or without escort, and had a bad time of it.

The *Betswood* was near the Nab, in company with some other ships. Her master, Captain J. H. Potts, thought there must have been several hundred German aircraft – although it was nothing like as bad as it seemed, for many of the planes were fighters. But what happened was still sufficiently spectacular. 'The scene changed,' he said, 'in an instant, from a perfectly flat sea to a typhoon.'

The *Betswood* was a small collier of 1,350 tons, just over 200 feet long. At this time, her sole armament was a single Lewis gun on the bridge. She steamed through untouched, as if she bore a charmed life. She was one of the few colliers of the 'Coal-Scuttle Brigade' to survive the war and she was to gain in the end the Channel 'Blue Riband' for making more wartime passages of the Straits of Dover than any other merchant ship. Her master was awarded the M.B.E.

The battle raged for several hours, between the Nab and Dunnose, a great cliff on the south shore of the Isle of Wight, until all this stretch of sea was littered with sinking and damaged ships. Some ships were hit, time after time.

The collier *Empire Crusader* was struck simultaneously by a bomb which hit the foredeck and another which exploded in the sea, two or three feet away, punching the water at her with crushing force and making her destruction certain. As she reeled from the shock, flames leapt up from the cargo – a bomb had landed in the coal, blown a crater in it, and splintered the hatches to matchwood. The mainmast was down, the engine room sky-lights broken and all the steam pipes burst. The whole front of the bridge had been blown in and the Second Mate was lying on the deck, seriously wounded. The Germans continued to attack.

Down below, amid the scalding chaos of escaping steam, Chief Engineer Joseph Cowper stopped the ship's engines; then he went up to the bridge, to see if there were any survivors. He found the Second Mate lying in the wreckage, too badly wounded to move. He called to an Able Seaman, William Robson, and together they began to carry the heavy body of the badly-injured man across the skylight towards one of the lifeboats. As they struggled with their load, the Germans were diving on the ship, machine-gunning it. There was a sudden series of tearing slaps – a brief whine ending in a whip-crack – and Robson stumbled, hit by a bullet.

The *Empire Crusader* was rolling sluggishly, and was very low in the water; there was no time for further search, and not much hope even if there had been time. Cowper went back to the lifeboat; it went running down into the water; and they pulled away from their sinking, burning ship. For the officers, and for many of the crew, a ship is their home; it is sad to see it go, even when it isn't taking the bodies of your friends down with it.

There were a good many tragedies like that, that day, for scattered over many miles of sea, under the chalk cliffs of the Isle of Wight and perfectly visible from shore, ten merchantmen were caught by the bombers. Two were caught alone, without any ship near them and without escort of any kind; they foundered, in a flurry of spray. The *Coquetdale* and the *Ajax* had gone to join the *Empire Crusader* on the seabed. The water was littered with cripples, stopped and drifting helplessly – or crawling slowly back to St Helen's Roads. They were not all British ships, as their names indicate – the *John M*, the *Scheldt*, the *Balmaha*, the *Veenenburgh*, the *Omlandia*, the *Surte*, and the *Tres*. The *Tres* was Norwegian, one of the many foreign ships whose captains had come to England rather than serve the Germans. A tug put out from Portsmouth dockyard to take her in tow; she was brought in to St Helen's Roads, so shattered that she sank at her moorings the following night.

But the casualties were not only to the merchantmen. The dive-bombers, roaming over the area at will, picked out the armed trawlers and armed yachts which had been part of the escort or had been sent out from Portsmouth to reinforce it. One of these was *H.M.S. Wilna*.

The *Wilna* was a rich man's toy – a powerful, converted motor yacht of 450 tons. Her main armament, like that of the trawlers, was an old-fashioned 4-inch gun designed to engage surface targets only; it would not elevate beyond 45 degrees. It could engage an aircraft flying low down some distance away, but since the shells were fitted with percussion fuses, they would explode only if they hit the aircraft directly – a million to one chance. Against dive-bombers there wasn't a chance at all, for the gun wouldn't bear. The *Wilna* brought to the battle only her anti-aircraft armament – a twin Lewis. 1914 against 1940.

She rounded Bembridge Ledge, with Culver Cliff rising out of the sea to starboard, and came across traces of the battle. She passed a water-logged lifeboat; it was riddled with bullet holes, woodwork gashed and splintered; and it was empty. Another half-sunken object floated by – a ship's wheelhouse. Off Dunnose lay an escort trawler, the *Kingston Chrysoberyl*; and no other ship in sight. There was only the wreckage, drifting half awash among the waves.

All this time the Germans had been booming about overhead, the deep, undulating growl of their motors striking down from the heights; from time to time there were bursts of machine-gun fire and the sheet-tearing noise of diving fighters. A sudden commotion directly overhead caused the crew of the *Wilna* to look up and then dive flat on the deck. As the 4-inch gun would not bear, the gun's crew lay down, too. Everyone, except the man behind the twin Lewis, lay flat. And he, squinting up into the sun, saw a stepped-up line of bombers heaving as if it had been kicked. Wings gleaming in the sunlight, the stukas peeled off, one by one, from 10,000 feet and came plunging down with a rushing roar, a kind of shrilling thunder made of engine noise and the howl of air round the dive-brakes. The noise broke no bones, but it was terrifying to hear. The twin Lewis clattered its reply.

The sea around the *Wilna* exploded in great gouts from the bombs and in hundreds of smaller splashes where splinters of bomb casing tore upwards to the surface. There were no direct hits, only near-misses, but the bombs bursting close alongside sent a shower of splinters tearing through the *Wilna* at deck level. The carpenter was lying face downwards on the planking – a bomb fragment, ripping through the low bulwarks, tore him open from chest to belly. Bullets and cannon shells sprayed the yacht. On the bridge was a box-like air-raid shelter, for just such an emergency as this – but a bullet went in, and took a man through the head. The nerve-wracking howl of dive-bombers and the tornado-thunder of the explosions seemed, to the *Wilna's* men, to last for ten minutes; but it was probably much less than that. Then the stukas were haring for home.

The *Wilna* lay stopped in the water, drifting helplessly under Dunnose, with her mast over the side, three men dead and six wounded. Two of the wounded were in extreme agony; if they were to live they needed skilled medical attention at once. There was no chance of rowing them ashore – the lifeboat seemed to consist more of holes than of planking, though it was later patched up. They looked across at the *Kingston Chrysoberyl*, but she had been attacked at the same time and was lying stopped, half hidden in a cloud of steam.

While they gave what attention they could to their own wounded, the *Wilna's* men waited for a tug and gave thanks that their ship was not coal-fired. The scenes aboard the *Kingston Chrysoberyl*, which was a coal-burner, were horrifying; with steam bursting up from below through every nook and cranny, every gap opened by the bombs – and the screaming of terribly scalded men. The bursting of the steam pipes had meant a terrible death for many of the crew, and her casualties were much heavier than those of the *Wilna*.

Her companion ship, the *Kingston Olivine*, suffered in much the same way, as did two other armed trawlers, the *Cape Palliser* and the *Stella Capella*, as well as another armed yacht, the *Rion*. The reason they lost so heavily was that they were all equipped as anti-submarine vessels, not flak ships (a later innovation). And this, in turn, was because of the sudden appearance of the Germans on the Channel, forcing us to a type of war we were not ready to deal with. In fact, the Channel was hardly used by German submarines, being something of a deathtrap for them on account of its shallow depths and the presence of so many small craft equipped for anti-submarine work; indeed, the U-boat was not a factor to be reckoned with by the coastal convoys.

All that day the Portsmouth tugs were going out to the damaged ships and bringing them into the Dockyard for repair. The losses, for that day's work around the Isle of Wight, were in all three ships sunk and 13 damaged, as well as three sunk and two damaged by or because of E-boats between Beachy Head and the Nab during the morning hours of darkness. It was a formidable total. Seen in perspective, the day's work was a nasty knock – but it was nothing like a knock-out blow.

Fighter Command had been out over the battle, though the ships were largely unaware of it, No. 145 Hurricane Squadron bearing the brunt of the fighting. At 11.45, for instance, they had been told to head off German aircraft coming in over Beachy Head, found six Me 110s there, were then informed over the R/T that there was a battle going on south of the Isle of Wight, and altered course in that direction. It took them ten minutes to get there; they saw the convoy, but no Germans. Later, they did intercept, and one pilot saw that a German pilot had joined the mêlée of crippled ships; he was sitting in his dinghy, looking rather lonely, the water around him tinged green by the release of chemicals carried to aid recognition and rescue.

The Air Ministry communiqué claimed that 400 German aircraft had taken part in the day's operations against the ships, and that 60 had been destroyed for the loss of 16 British fighters. The actual exchange rate was 28 German aircraft and 20 British. And on 11th August there were further attacks on convoys, as well as on Dover and Portland, with air losses very nearly equal – 35 German to 32 British.*

* *The Royal Air Force 1939–1945*, Vol. I (H.M.S.O.).

The German claims of shipping losses inflicted on the British were astronomical. The IX Air Group alone reported that they had sunk 950,000 tons, by direct attack and by minelaying, by 31st July.* This Group was a part only of Luftflotte 2, which was in turn a part only of the Luftwaffe. In fact, sinkings by mine were heavier than those by any other cause; but, though the losses by direct attack had risen sharply, they were still only 24,000 tons during the period 10th July–7th August. Nevertheless, during the peak phase of the Battle of the Channel, the coastal convoys had lost on an average one third of their number, sunk or damaged beyond repair.†

This ordeal for their crews was now over, for on the following day, 12th August, the Battle of Britain began. The fight was pushed beyond the convoys, to the ports and coastal aerodromes; and then, much later, inland; and finally, to London. The convoys were to be attacked in the future, sometimes heavily, but never again were they to be so consistently the target; to sail through no man's sea, in front of our own barbed wire, while the enemy's preliminary barrage beat down on them, their protection virtually limited to that of their own guns.

* The Memoirs of Field-Marshal Kesselring, p. 63.
† The War at Sea, Vol. I, pp. 324–6 (H.M.S.O.).

As the bombers and fighters of Air Fleets 2 and 3 droned back
from the first day of the all-out assault on England, there was
a momentary series of flashes from the French coast opposite
Dover – winking sheets of light, gone in an instant. They came
from heavy guns. The muzzles were not pointed at Dover – but
reared up almost vertically. The projectiles slammed upwards,
far above the bombers, reached the top of their arc – miles high –
and began to slant downwards. They fell into Dover much faster
than the sound of their passage.

There was no warning; no howl or whistle. Merely a heavy
crraack! The earth trembled. And three or four billowing towers
of smoke and dust rose up above the houses. Dover was under
shellfire.

These were ranging shots. Batteries were being set up on the
opposite cliffs, and as they came into position, so they fired
ranging shots at the most obvious target – the nearest town on
the other side of the Straits. For some batteries it was Dover, for
others Folkestone. There was no barrage yet.

Elsewhere, the German blitzkrieg had fallen upon small countries with stunning force; the blows appearing to be delivered with
brutal confidence and power, helping to build up the legend of
German invincibility. It did seem, to neutrals many thousands of
miles away, that nothing could stop the Wehrmacht; that their
onrush was irresistible; that unprepared England must go down
before them like a stunned calf. In terms of fireworks, the first
day of the assault had been spectacular. Clouds of smoke and
dust blotting out the arrogant face of England, bomb flashes
winking like fireflies across the docks and aerodromes, shaking
the comfortable islanders out of their centuries-old invincible
calm. So it seemed to the German crews as, hot with the taste
of death and danger, they flew back at noon under the high sun.
It had been a breathless business for them; not so easy as attacking under-armed and ill-escorted convoys out of range of the
shore guns. The rocketting plunge of the dive-bombers had been
shaken by the opposition. Not much, for those pilots had verve

and courage, but enough to make all the difference in pin-point bombing such as this.

In battle, men are both excited and afraid at the same time – a delicate and precarious balance. The one thing they never tell of their experiences is the cold, sober truth; because they are neither cold nor sober – but highly charged with emotion.

There had been no weight behind the attack – only about 30 bombers directed at Portsmouth, with perhaps 10 more for the Isle of Wight, and the bombers themselves carried a comparatively light bomb-load. It was a rapier attack, and everything depended on getting the point home.

There was no comparison whatever between this and the later Allied attacks by between one and two thousand British and American aircraft, carrying much heavier bomb-loads. With these, it hardly mattered where the bombs fell, as long as they fell on the right city – sometimes they didn't – because the 'carpet' of bombs would take care of everything. Their greatest success, in terms of death roll, was at Dresden, where 70,000 people were killed in a series of attacks spread over 14 hours. The Germans' best effort in this line had been Rotterdam, with 25,000 killed in $2\frac{1}{2}$ hours. The civilian casualties in Portsmouth, on 'Eagle Day', amounted to 13 killed.

It was a matter, not only of weight, but of method. The Germans were not, at this point, interested in causing civilian casualties; rightly, they believed that it paid better to hit the nerve centres – but they had hit only one, the radar station on the Isle of Wight, and that was soon repaired; they had near-missed the others. Their aircrews, fascinated by the evidence of fires and explosions, went back to report success; and the process of self-delusion began.

But for Dover, 12th August was a significant date. On the sea-front now is a plaque presented to the town by the people of Calais; it had been taken from a German gun, part of the Sangatte Battery, and on it the gun's crew had recorded their score. They had fired 2,224 shells at the Dover *area* – that is, at the town and at convoys passing Dover. The town, and the convoys, were now to be shelled consistently for four years.

Although Dover is officially credited with being the first target, there were mysterious explosions in Folkestone some days before 12th August. There were rumours of shell-fire whispered in the town – whispered because it might be thought that they were spreading 'alarm and despondency'.

For ten days, from 12th August, ranging shots were fired

across the Straits. Then, on 22nd August, appeared the apparently perfect target. A convoy of eighteen ships, creeping along close inshore at little more than the pace of a man walking. They were moving up channel, bound for Southend. The Germans opened up, for the first time, with a barrage, the convoy being passed on from battery to battery as it moved slowly through the Straits.

There was no warning; merely the thud-crraack! of the shells bursting – and great, towering columns of water rising high above the ships, spreading, falling, subsiding in a swirling vortex; with splinters whining away out of the spume and smoke.

Some of the sailors scanned the sky, looking for the bombers which, they thought, must have taken them unawares; others, catching sight of flashes winking from the vicinity of Boulogne, assumed that the R.A.F. were out in daylight, hammering the invasion fleet. There had been two groups of three flashes. A minute later, with a rumbling roar and flash, six geysers sprang up alongside and in front of the ship. 'Never mind,' said one Master, 'they never put 'em in the same place twice.'

It was a beautiful day, with long lines of marching clouds that sent long dark ripples of shadow across the calm sea. A ripple of flashes from the French coast – a count of 50 or 60 seconds – the winking red heart of the shellbursts – and once again the columns of water, rising up, stately, dreadful, and subsiding in upon themselves with a final splash upon the water.

Destroyers tore down the columns, making smoke; and the dark clouds pouring from their funnels rolled slowly over the water, masking the slowly-driving ships; and the guns still firing, at long, spaced intervals, into the smokescreen, salvo after salvo. As the Boulogne batteries fell silent, the range lengthening, the Calais guns took up the barrage. It was a long drawn out ordeal for the merchantmen.

To the Germans, the day must have been a great disappointment. The guns had not been installed in order to sink colliers; they were there as part of the invasion plan. Their task was, in the absence of a substantial German surface fleet, to close the sea flanks of the beachhead. The first wave might well get across without opposition. Indeed, the Royal Navy made no rash promises to stop it. What they did promise was to cut it off from all reinforcements and supply, so that the first wave would wither in the beachhead like a flower snipped off at the stalk.

The German invasion fleets were a laughable improvisation on Gallipoli lines; if the Navy got among the fat troopships and clumsy barges, the disaster would rival Gallipoli. The German heavy batteries were set up to prevent this, by sinking or driving off all British ships trying to interfere with the proposed sea-borne conveyor belt between the Pas de Calais and Kent. With the help of the 'Flying Artillery', which had now been withdrawn from the battle – partly because of losses, partly to assist in this operation – and with the additional aid of minefields, the Germans really thought they could close the flanks of the beach-head and bar the Straits to all comers, though their main targets would be thirty or so fast destroyers.

Now the guns, in their first shoot, had clean missed a large convoy of dead-slow colliers steaming slowly and in formation under the cliffs of Dover. They had fired 145 rounds at ships steaming at 6 or 7 knots; they hadn't hit them, they hadn't even stopped them, or thrown them out of formation. The unharmed passage of the 'Coal-Scuttle Brigade' cast serious doubts on the practicability of the entire invasion plan.

Also, the English fired back. A single 14-inch gun, on the cliffs above Dover, it represented no real threat to them; but it was a warning that, if they wanted to come, they were not in for a quiet stroll through the Kentish countryside. They could huff and puff, but unless they could blow the house down, there was little chance of occupying it. And this was a very poor return for all their efforts, which were considerable.

From August, 1940, until early in 1943, gun salvoes were a regular, nerve-wracking and expected feature of the passage. They were still firing in August, 1944, but with less enthusiasm. It really was very difficult to hit a small ship at a range of twenty miles. Also, the rifling of the barrels wore out very quickly and were expensive to replace. The cost of keeping a convoy under fire throughout the passage of the Straits was something over £100,000.

Dover, being larger, was easier to hit, and a good deal of damage was done; in September alone, it was shelled six times; on the worst day, the 9th, over 150 rounds were fired. But, as the population was down to about one-fifth of its pre-war level, casualties were not in proportion. However, in spite of its four-year ordeal, the town was not reduced to a heap of rubble, or anything like it.

Shellfire is not at all the same thing as bombing. To start with, a shell is not dropped, it is fired. To stand the shock of the discharge, it must have a strong, thick casing – it therefore contains a smaller amount of explosive, for its size and weight, than a bomb; and the explosive, before it can get to work on a house or a ship, has first to blow open the thick casing, thus wasting part of its force unproductively. The splinters, naturally, are much more solid than those from a bomb casing.

The real talking point of the gun is not explosive power but accuracy; and not merely accuracy, but repetitive accuracy. Once a battery has the range, they can keep putting 90 per cent of their shots slap on it until they run out of ammunition or the barrels wear out. And of all gunnery, coastal gunnery is the most accurate, because the gun platform is stable and its position known. Nevertheless, the guns on both sides of the Straits, British and German, rarely hit each other's convoys.

The gun is a delicate, precision weapon – very costly to make – unlike the blundering bomb; but its accuracy falls off markedly at extreme range. And Dover, and the swept channel outside, were at extreme range even for the most powerful of the German guns.

It was this sort of projectile which fell around the colliers, with their wafer-thin sides, and into Dover – on to houses and not on to massive armour plate. It was a terribly destructive, penetrative force – but limited in area. In proportion to the weight, there was not much blast. The shell went deep before exploding, then spent a great deal of its energy on earth or water.

It had one other awkward characteristic – there could be no preliminary warning, such as the siren for an air raid;* and no warning from the projectile itself. You simply couldn't hear it coming – not, that is, when it was coming at you.

This was the measure of the ordeal suffered by Dover and her slowly-passing ships for four years. At any time, wherever you were and whatever you were doing, you might be wiped out, or maimed, without even the few seconds' warning scream of a bomb or an ordinary shell which gave you just enough time to drop flat or dive for cover. In Dover, there was no cessation of strain; you were in danger all the time – for four years. People did make a joke of it, but it was really no joke.

The strain, in a collier passing the Straits, was far greater; not only were they powerless, but they were the actual target; and for those down below it was worse than for those on deck. Working amid the gleaming, thumping machinery and surrounded by steam pipes, with only wafer-thin plates between them and the sea outside, they did not know when they would be fired at, only that they *would* be fired at. When the shells arrived, they could

* Dover did have a 'shell-warning' but only after the first salvo had arrived.

40

hear and feel the shock of them through the hull; and they knew that if the ship was hit they would instantly have the flesh stripped off their bones by the explosion of the super-heated steam; if by some chance they survived, perhaps terribly scalded and blind, there was still the long climb to the upper deck.

No ship that continually passed the Straits could long escape damage. The *Betswood*, which did the trip more times than any other collier, was several times damaged. The nearest she came to final disaster was off Dover, when two shells pitched close alongside, bursting twenty feet above the water with a red flash. She came to a stop, burning, with thirty holes ripped in her hull and superstructure.

Her master, Captain J. H. Potts, stopped his engines and then ordered the damage control partly over the side. As they got their ladders out, he listed the *Betswood*, to bring the underwater damage above the surface of the sea. The collier lay in the Straits, heeled over and drifting, as the crew swarmed down the ladders laid over the side, with mallets and wooden plugs, and began hammering them into the jagged gaps torn in the plating by the hot steel. Meanwhile, in the blazing magazine, a tragicomedy was taking place.

The fire-precaution in the magazine was a sprinkler; in order to work it, a man had to get on top of the magazine, and risk being blown sky-high while he did it. The man detailed to work the sprinkler was a member of the crew. He took one look at the proposition and declined. 'Not my ammo,' he said. 'That's Navy ammo, that is; let them look after it. Not my job.'

The magazine continued to burn furiously and a ship's officer pointing out that a little more time wasted in argument would see them all trying to get past St Peter. 'All right,' flung out the sailor, as he disappeared into the blaze and smoke of the magazine. 'But I'm doing it under protest, mind.' And do it he did.

After she had repaired damage and put out the fire, the *Betswood* got the bone between her teeth again, and carried on down Channel to her destination.

For four years the ordeal went on, the ships usually steaming through the bursts from exploding shells, unscathed except for fittings and crockery broken by near-misses and holes punched in their sides by splinters. It was not until 1944 that Captain Potts, of the *Betswood*, saw a hit on another ship in the convoy.

The heavy shell pitched straight onto number three hatch, and then the collier vanished. There was a huge cloud of what looked like black smoke hanging low over the sea, and a patch of

41

furiously disturbed water below. The black smoke was not smoke at all – it was coal dust, blown hundreds of feet up from the explosion of the 15-inch shell in the hold. Of the collier there was no sign, she had gone completely and instantaneously, with all her crew.

On the British side, too, heavy guns were installed; and, in 1940, there was something of a race to see who would be able to open fire 'firstest with the mostest'.

Under Churchill's spur the Navy, and to a lesser extent, the Army rapidly fortified the Straits. By the beginning of September, a 14-inch Naval gun had been added, as well as two 9.2-inch railway guns and four smaller Naval guns. The old battleship *Iron Duke* had been bombed and beached at Scapa; two 13.5-inch guns were taken out of her and set up at Dover on railway mountings, as well as four 5.5-inch guns from the battlecruiser *Hood*. But, for every gun Churchill whipped into position, the Germans set up ten; and by the time Churchill's guns were ready, to fire them would be to court an altogether unequal duel.

Even without an invasion, these guns were frequently in action, barring our side of the Straits to E-boats in daylight and making life hazardous for the minelayers which used to slip across and try to mine the swept channel used by the convoys. The E-boats did try several times to repeat the attack they had made on 25th July, when the destroyers had been there to see them off. Now, there were no destroyers, but the shellfire so upset them that, unsure of what was happening, they began to fire among themselves. After that, they transferred their operations east and west of the Straits.

As radar developed, fire could be opened on unseen targets in bad visibility or at night. One cloudy day in 1942 the sets picked up signs of shipping movement in the deep-water channels on the other side of the Straits, so much of it that something big was clearly about to happen. Then the coast-watching set at Fairlight burnt out a valve, and the screen went dark. A R.E.M.E. officer was sent in some haste to Fairlight, carrying a replacement valve. On the lonely Romney Marshes his car broke down. The *Scharnhorst*, *Gneisnau* and *Prince Eugen* were coming up Channel at 32 knots, but he didn't know that. Nevertheless, when an Army lorry full of infantry passed him, he stopped it, bundled out the infantry, got in and tore across the marsh for Fairlight, leaving the stranded infantry standing in the middle of the marsh, cursing all 'bloody officers'.

The set came on again in time to pick up the three big German ships and their escort – they were in range for precisely 17 minutes. In that time, 33 rounds were fired at them from Dover, but, though they landed near the ships, there were no hits.

Later, two 15-inch guns were installed – 'Jane' and 'Clem' – which were to score on demand, a most amazing bulls-eye, at a range of over 40,000 yards – they got a direct hit on one of their opposite numbers sited on the French coast.

5 · A Shilling a Month

'This 'ere's the hoven door –
Number two hopens the hoven –
Number three slams dinner into hoven –
Number one squeezes the trigger,
Hand away goes the fucking dinner!'

THE instructor paused. 'Got that?' The group of men round the 12-pdr nodded. Sometimes they would be Naval ratings – young men, obviously 'Hostiles' (Hostilities Only), or older men, with 'Royal Fleet Reserve' on their cap bands; or Marines. And sometimes they would be civilians – men of the Merchant Navy. In any case the drill – and the 'patter' – was much the same. Defensive Equipment, Merchant Ships was in operation.

Technically, a merchant ship should be defensively armed only, otherwise she was liable to internment in any neutral port; and defensive armament, by long usage, fired astern – at a pursuer. This was old when Nelson was young.

The rule was that the guns of a merchant ship must not be able to fire 'abaft the beam' – in other words, the guns could fire, roughly, broadside and astern, but not ahead. D.E.M.S. had to find the guns, fit them, and then find gunners to serve them.

To begin with, most of the guns came from store – where they had lain, heavily greased, ever since 1918; and the men to man them came from the merchant navy, members of the ship's crew, with perhaps a Naval pensioner shipped aboard to train them, or an ex-Marine. The crew members chosen would be those who were least essential to the working of the ship – the steward, for instance.

After three weeks' training he passed as seaman gunner; and after a further ten days, as gunlayer. In peacetime, in the Royal Navy, that process would have taken five years. When the battlefront moved to the Channel, the training was cut still further; large numbers of gunners were wanted, and quickly. In practice, this sometimes meant that a civilian would report to a Naval Barracks on the Monday, get his hair cut on the Tuesday, be documented, kitted and jagged, and on the Saturday put on a train to a Naval gunnery school. There he would receive two weeks' training in the theory of gunnery, with a little practical handling weapons – mostly the heavier type which he would not in fact expect to use – from instructors who, though sound enough, had had their grounding in the first world war and were not particularly up-to-date on aircraft.

He would then be posted to a merchant ship, and signed on as a member of the crew – though wearing Naval uniform and receiving Naval pay – at the nominal rate of 'one shilling per month'. Everyone carried by a merchant ship must sign on – even the Captain's wife – and his children, if they accompany him.

The Naval rating now had to train some members of the crew to help him with his job of manning the guns; and it was extremely difficult for him. He was not a sailor – for he had never been to sea; he was, despite his uniform, no Jack Tar – for Naval tradition is not learnt in three weeks; and he had no discipline – for this, too, is not installed in three weeks; and he was hardly a gunner at all. And if the ship sailed in the morning, he might be in action in the afternoon.

If he was ever going to be an efficient gunner, he would have to learn the job in the face of the enemy; the triumphant enemy which had swept over all Europe, crumbling nations and armies into the dust; and his lessons were likely to be bitter ones.

Still, he looked like a sailor – and the nation has always had faith in its Navy. It was not misplaced.

In addition to fitting the merchantmen with guns and gunners, D.E.M.S. had to build accommodation for them, in a hurry; and despite the hurry, some colliers still retain these structures to this day, the crew having found them very useful. D.E.M.S. was the equivalent at sea of the Home Guard; except that the Home Guard never saw action, whereas D.E.M.S. sailed right into it. There hardly was a typical armament; they got what was going, when it was going – when they were in port. The turn-round of the ships could not be delayed for the benefit of D.E.M.S. – for that would reduce the convoy system to hopeless chaos. A Lewis was no great matter; but a heavier gun might need more time to install than was available – in that case, it might have to be fitted in stages.

In any case, the masters did not like it. When they looked at the guns, they saw – not protection from dive-bombers – but heavy weights, placed high up. The epitaph of many colliers, even today, reads simply: 'Last seen floating bottom upwards'. Colliers have always been dangerous ships, and they are dangerous still. The cargo is loose and in bulk; so that a heavy sea on the beam, consistently heeling the ship over more to one side than the other, will pile up the coal or coke on that side. The ship will take on a list; and if the sea continues and nothing is or can be done about moving the cargo, the list will increase until the ship turns over.

But it is not necessary for it to turn right over before disaster comes; for if the scuppers on one side are level with the water, the sea will break over the hatches; if they are not steel, it may break them in. The hatches are always the vulnerable point with colliers – to allow of rapid discharging they are much larger than in other merchant ships. The gradual introduction of steel hatches had one important bearing on the war – a ship so fitted which was struck by an E-boat's torpedo usually remained in one piece, even if it eventually sank; whereas a collier with wooden hatches usually broke in two, and went down like two halves of a stone.

The D.E.M.S. ratings came aboard – and like as not found other gunners already there; these were the Merchant Navy Gunners who were picked from the crews of merchant ships to help man the guns. They wore a peaked cap and an armband as their 'uniform'. The prestige accorded among sailors to a peaked cap can hardly be realised by landsmen, particularly if it goes with a jacket and brass buttons.

D.E.M.S. ratings had been in the Navy only a short time – hardly long enough to learn its traditions and thoroughly identify themselves with it; they looked like sailors, but they didn't feel like it. And some had been told to take over the gun in style; to hold proper drills – to fall in the gun's crew smartly, number them off, and generally put a spark in it.

The nation had not been prepared to pay, in peacetime, for a powerful Navy; and, in wartime, it did not get one. Not, at any rate, to begin with. And in comparison with the Navy, the needs of the coasters had to take second place. Besides this, by a series of miscalculations remote from the ships, Hitler was now on the Channel instead of locked behind the Rhine.

That sparked off in turn a trail of events which was to bring two types of gunner into the coastal convoys; both of these came under D.E.M.S., but were sharply distinct from the D.E.M.S. gunners who were posted, as we have seen, to a particular ship and stayed in that ship all the time, teaching members of the crew to assist them in handling the fixed armament of the ship.

Both organisations came into being during the Battle of Britain, as a direct result of the slaughter of the convoys; so that the guns' crews of a collier, by September 1940, might be made up of Naval ratings serving permanently with the ship; Naval ratings who just came along for the trip, and brought their guns and ammunition with them; infantrymen who did the same; supernumerary members of the crew enrolled as Merchant Navy Gunners in their own ship; and anyone else who felt like lending a hand, and had the time for it. It might seem that Fred Karno had gone to sea.

The scene around the guns of a collier would have provided a splendidly amusing situation with which to begin a West End farce. But it wasn't a West End farce; it wasn't a farce of any kind. It was the future of the world.

The German Army had broken every one of its opponents at lightning speed and with confident ease; the coal-scuttle helmets had reached the Channel. What the Kaiser could not achieve in five years, Hitler had accomplished in five weeks.

It is hard now to recapture the magic invincibility which then clothed the Wehrmacht. It was the high point of German arms: the peak – did he but know it – of the Führer's career. From now, the road led downward, into the shadows, to the bunker near the Brandenburg Gate. The Germans could be stopped.

But we did not know it then.

6 · *The Channel Guard*

A COLLIER master has left a description of A.A. Guard gunners coming on board his ship at Southend. The convoy was due to sail at two o'clock in the afternoon. At one o'clock precisely an officer brought them aboard. There were four of them, carrying their kit, their bedding, their Lewis guns and their ammunition. They were Cockneys, cheery, quick-witted, at home anywhere. They dumped their kit on the deck, clamped their guns to the rail with a special gadget made for the purpose; they looked around the deck, saw that the cargo of coke was higher than the hatchways, and borrowed shovels from the crew. Then they began to dig.

In a few minutes they had dug themselves foxholes in the coke, curled themselves up on deck by their guns – and were asleep.

These were the men who probably saw more action than anyone else, for they did more trips than anyone else. In his wallet, each man carried a card given to him by his unit before leaving to join his first convoy. The card bore, approximately, the following message:

'When you go aboard this vessel, you will say to yourself: "I am the Navy." Throw out your chest, go immediately to your gun and make ready. Never leave your gun at any time.'

Experience had shown, that if a man did leave his gun for any reason, and there was an attack, he never got back to it in time to be of use. So they slept by their guns, in the one hour that was left to them before the convoy sailed.

It would be a 'night on the tiles' for everyone, and they wanted to be fresh for it. The master knew about D.E.M.S., of course, but this batch were new to him. Later, he came down from his bridge for a moment to talk to them. Two of the men were from Carter Paterson, one was a butcher, the other a pitman; none of them had been in the Navy for more than a few months, but they were strikingly well-disciplined and keen, and obviously knew their job. Their unit, the A.A. Guard, was as brand new as they were.

They had come from its headquarters in Portsmouth, as

anti-aircraft protection to a ship sailing in convoy from Spithead to Southend; now they were going back in this ship. They did the run three or four times a week, never spending more than 48 hours ashore either at Portsmouth or at Southend. Accommodation was still a little rough; in fact, at Southend there wasn't any. They were fed in a requisitioned hotel, but slept on the pier – that is to say, on the boards of the pier.

No two men will ever give exactly the same account of a battle, but here the evidence was unanimous – those boards were hard.

They took their guns with them because, after Dunkirk – with the Army crying out for machine-guns to defend the country against invasion – there were not enough to go round all the merchant ships, which spent a good deal of their time in port, loading and discharging, or just hanging around waiting for a convoy to form. To make a few guns go a long way, they were simply moved from ship to ship, and the ammunition for them. If this convoy had not been sailing, they would have returned to Portsmouth by train, with their guns and ammunition, in the hope of picking up a convoy from there.

The A.A. Guard was formed as a direct result of the hammering received by C.W.8 on 'Black Thursday'. It was obvious now that the Channel convoys were a special case, taking for the moment the brunt of the German onslaught; their defence called for an efficiency in the gunners far above that needed normally in other areas, where a gunner might perhaps get in an occasional shot at a surfaced submarine or long-range bomber. A Channel convoy was certain to be attacked; and, as 'forcing the Straits' was now a naval operation, it must get through. And that meant thickening up the A.A. defence; to pack the colliers with as many A.A. guns as possible, manned by men as highly trained as possible.

It was not until early in September 1940 that the A.A. Guard was ready for action because, if they were to be effective, their training had to be exceptionally thorough. After going through a normal gunnery course at Whale Island, they went to Eastney ranges for anti-aircraft training – both of these establishments being at Portsmouth. The address of the 180 ratings of the Guard was: the Infants' School, Northern Parade, Southsea; newcomers were always thunderstruck when entering the lavatories for the first time – the seats were so low. And the view – from the seat – was unusual. Tacked to the door, facing them, was a celluloid sheet of aircraft silhouettes, so that they could brush up their aircraft recognition at the same time.

While the A.A. Guard was still forming, an anchored convoy had been caught off the Motherbank. This was the convoy assembly area between Ryde and Lee-on-Solent, only a few miles from Portsmouth. There had been no dive-bombing, no warning. The aircraft had come boring in just over the sea, wave-hopping towards the ships – they had rocketted over the mastheads before the gun's crews knew what was happening; and by that time, it was much too late. Half the convoy had been sunk.

The natural reaction of many recruits was to be afraid of a gun – afraid of being hurt by the kick. Any loose, nervous holding of the gun will leave the man's shoulder black and blue with bruises; it will also leave the target unscathed. The men had to be trained to *feel* offensive, to swing the gun and fire as fast and effortlessly as a farmer will handle a shot-gun, for that was the sort of shooting it was. A countryman, who had probably done a fair amount of poaching in his time, would present no problem – he was ideal material for short-range A.A. work. A Birmingham bank clerk, on the other hand, might take much longer to learn, and be disconcerted if there were any doubt about whether or not to fire.

Because the offensive spirit had been so thoroughly instilled into its officers and men, the A.A. Guard once accounted for an R.A.F. flying boat from Calshot.

By the spring of 1941 the Channel Guard had proved so successful in protecting coasters on the run Southend–Southampton that their activities were extended to all merchant ships on passage as far west as Falmouth. That in turn meant a reinforcement of 60 men and a search for new accommodation. It was found at Calmore, near Southampton, where too the men back from service in the Channel could get a good night's rest, instead of having to take shelter from air raids. This was the period of the heavy night blitzes, when the Luftwaffe struck at all the big seaports in turn.

The strength of the Channel Guard increased rapidly, finally reaching 400. Many of these men were dentally unfit – that is, they had false teeth. On the longer trips, which they were soon to take, it was unlikely that they would be closed up at the guns all the time; some would go below to sleep – and the first thing a man does, before he goes to sleep, is to take out his false teeth. Then, ten to one, if the alarm goes, he dashes to his gun without them – and is a casualty before he starts.

By July 1941, the emergency in the Channel was over, and the Canadian officers who had seen the Guard through the worst of the fighting were released; in most cases being able to pick the job they wanted. Their places were taken by young R.N.V.R. officers. At the beginning of the New Year, the Guard took on new commitments in merchant ships sailing from the Bristol Channel to Liverpool and Belfast; and in June 1942 they went even further afield.

It was a very mysterious affair at first. Their commander, Commander Spencer, received a telephone message: 'How many men have you got?' He replied: 'None – they're all at sea.' The reply came back: 'I want a draft of 18 men, with their officers. You provide them. They will catch the 7.50 from Euston tonight.'

'If any men come in within the next few hours, I'll send them straight away,' was Commander Spencer's reply. And some of them did come in, at the very last moment, tired and hungry after seeing a convoy through. It was too late to catch the train from Southampton, they would have to go by road, and without a meal. With their guns and ammunition they were stowed into a car and a lorry – food, cigarettes, and beer bottles being slung in at them as the vehicles were actually moving off.

They had no idea where they were off to; even Commander Spencer didn't know, and the voice on the telephone wouldn't say. But the resourceful Chief Petty Officer in charge of the lorry had a good idea that, if he didn't do something, they would miss the train. As they entered the outskirts of London, he stopped the truck – outside a police station, and got swift action.

In a few minutes they were off – flat out through London – led by three police motor-cyclists.

The 7.50 left Euston that night at 7.55 – but the Channel Guard were on board. Few of them came back. The convoy was P.Q.17.

It was ironic that the Channel Guard, formed to defend the coastal colliers plying between Southend and Southampton, should at length send some of its officers and men to die in the Barents Sea. One or two of the survivors lost their feet, from frost-bite; the crew of the ship they were defending – not a British ship – took to the boats on the approach of the enemy, and before ever an attack was launched.

By this time the A.A. Guard had virtually worked themselves out of a job. After mid-1942 a serious air attack on a coastal convoy was a matter for surprise; there were not many German aircraft left in the West, and what there were, were wary. The convoys were prickly with guns and feeling aggressive. The Guard were disbanded, but *H.M.S. Safeguard* remained, as an

51

ideal central training depot for D.E.M.S. The Admiralty sent the Channel Guard a final signal which, for the professional Navy who are inclined to take efficiency and bravery rather for granted, was perhaps unique:

'The untiring effort and magnificent spirit of the Officers and men of the A.A. Guard in the defence of Coastal convoys over the past two years has been an inspiration to all. Though the A.A. Guard has now been absorbed in D.E.M.S., it is confidently felt that *Safeguard* in her new role as D.E.M.S. Depot will continue to instil that same spirit of efficiency and pride of Service in others.'

But perhaps their finest tribute lay simply in the statistics, which recorded that, though many ships were sunk under them by mine or torpedo, *the A.A. Guard never lost a ship to air attack.*

7 · Soldiers At Sea

THE Orderly Sergeant passed down the rows of bunks while two soldiers, blinking, wondered vaguely if there was time for a wash, shave, bootshine, and breakfast, in addition.

That morning the two soldiers, one of whom had been a London journalist, were in a truck – on their way to Southend and the 'dirtiest, rustiest, most down-at-heel old collier' they had ever set eyes on. The cook, who manned the collier's armament, a 'shaky old Lewis', was delighted to see them; and was soon giving them a brew in the galley.

Scenes like this, with variations, were being enacted in Infantry Battalions all over the country. One day, men would be square-bashing in some Army camp; the next day they might be on the deck of a coaster standing out of the Humber, with Spurn Head to port. The Navy had found another source of supply for the A.A. defence of merchant ships.

The first batch of 300 men were simply 'borrowed' by D.E.M.S. quite early in 1940. They were strictly on loan, for a few months; after that they would have to be returned. By July, when a real emergency had developed, their units were demanding them back; but the soldiers had done so well that D.E.M.S. was most unwilling to let them go. The decision to use them in the first place was anything but illogical. The need was not for sailors, but for expert light machine-gunners – and the Army or, more precisely, the infantry, had more of them than anyone else.

The organisation, if such it can be called – for it was then only a skeleton framework – was known simply as the 'A.A. Defence of Merchant Shipping'. It was commanded by a Major of the Scots Guards, with twelve liaison officers under him.

The first to be appointed was Captain F. A. Rundall, of the Royal Scots. On 20th February, 1940, he went to Methil – in peacetime, a loading port for colliers. Now, in wartime, not only was it the most northerly port of call for colliers, it was also the assembly point for convoys in the north. On 7th July, Lieutenant H. P. Stephenson, of the East Yorkshire Regiment, went to Hull to organise army gunners embarking or disembarking there; a number of the ships were colliers bound for or from the coal-loading port of Goole, further up the Humber. On 21st August, Second Lieutenant J. A. H. Peacoke, of the Queen's Regiment, went to Southend; and on 29th November Lieutenant R. C. S. Cooper, R.A., took up his duties at Tynemouth, which for a period of a few months replaced Methil as the main convoy assembly area on the north-east coast. The collier-loading port was Blyth, just north of the Tyne, from which the colliers steamed south to join the convoys near Newcastle.

These routes had been subject to attack by German aircraft flying on 'Armed Reconnaissance' almost since the beginning of the war. That part of the war was called the 'Phoney War' because there was no land fighting in the west and because civilians, by an unspoken, unwritten mutual agreement, were not being bombed. Shipping, since it did not involve the accidental killing of civilians on land, was regarded as a legitimate target which would not invoke retaliation on cities by the Not-So-Great Deterrent. The war off the east coast was by no means 'phoney'.

However, Hitler's impatience to be active on land – and the fact that while Germany had a powerful bomber force we had an exceedingly weak one – eventually nullified the unspoken agreement.

But Dowding never allowed anyone to dictate his battle for him, and he rotated his squadrons; those which were tired and decimated, he rested – and he rested them in the north. They met Stumpff's bombers and long-range fighters out to sea. Very few got through to Tyneside. The Germans discovered, that day, that the Me 110 was not to be compared to the Me 109; it was almost a matter of fighter versus bomber, with the odds very much on the fighter. Their losses exceeded acceptable limits, and it was clear that daylight action by the Luftwaffe on any scale was possible only within the very limited range of cover by the Me 109s. That meant the south-east; but roving bombers in cloudy weather could still range the north coast – and shipping badly needed the protection of the army gunners.

The men took to it like ducks to water. Theoretically, these men were soldiers; in the same way that, theoretically, the D.E.M.S. ratings were sailors. In fact, many of them had been in the Army a matter of two or three weeks and had got no further than an Initial Training Centre. They had been introduced to the rifle, could name the parts of the Bren, done a little bayonet drill, and some square bashing. It is not true that the first nine years of

Army life are the worst, but the first few weeks or months certainly are; they had experienced the Army at its worst, and they did not like it. They were glad to get away.

The spectacle of soldiers taking to the sea was not really novel. In fact, there was a direct comparison with Elizabethan times.

By August 1940 teams of 20 gunners were allotted to most of the major ports engaged in the coastal trade, as a Pool. By November more men, guns and equipment were pouring in. Even in a crisis such as this, the baser elements of human nature were at work below the surface.

The training, at first sketchy because of lack of equipment, later became excellent; with Dome Teachers, films, and target practice at drogues towed by aircraft. There was also a certain amount of boatwork, so that the men would not be complete novices at sea. To ensure that men put on their own in civilian surroundings shouldn't slack off, there was an N.C.O. in each gun team – one man at least who had something to lose. If there were only two gunners, one would be a lance-jack. If there were six, probably a sergeant would be in charge. But if there were only two gunners, and both private soldiers, one of them would be promoted on the spot. Promotion was rapid and, because the officers at that time did not know their men very well, it was a difficult problem. To a certain extent, they had to guess.

In January, still another category of gunner was added to the already long list of those serving in merchant ships – these were the Port Gunners. Their job was to guard the ship while in harbour, mainly as a precaution against sabotage. As the A.A. gunners came off the ship, they went on; and vice versa. The experiment did not last very long, because there were in fact no saboteurs.

Hull, particularly, was a frequent target – it was more frequently attacked than anywhere else, and the attacks continued long after they had died down elsewhere. The basic reason was that it was not only our third largest port, but it was also easy to find. Kesselring's bomber crews, roving off the east coast on the look-out for shipping, would unload on Hull if the seas proved to be empty or the ships hidden by bad visibility. New aircrews, doing their first few operations or training navigators, would be sent to Hull – the easy target. And if the weather closed in on targets further inland, then the bomber crews would be diverted – to Hull. Night after night, the bombs came whining down, the ships in the harbour ringed with fire from the blazing port installations. Next day, the newspapers would report a raid on a 'North East Coast Town'. Almost invariably, it was Hull. And through all this, and in spite of it, the gunners had to be got to and from the merchant ships lying at the heart of the target area.

In May 1941 the organisation was taken over by the Royal Artillery, the officers and men being formed into Regiments and Batteries while continuing to do their job at sea and on shore. Their new name was the Maritime Royal Artillery and, from a small emergency force of infantrymen serving only in coastal convoys, the expansion was rapid. At the end of the war, there were six Regiments, each of about 2,500 men, one based in India; they served in every merchant ship, from colliers to 'Queens', in every ocean in the world. The Memorial to one Regiment alone contains the names of more than 400 killed or drowned at sea.

It has been said that, while few Englishmen are 'born soldiers', every Englishman is at heart a sailor. They proved the truth of it.

8 · *Eagle Squadron Strikes*

By 4th June, 1940, the Germans were on the Channel coast. They were very surprised to be there. Operation YELLOW had succeeded far beyond the directive, which had originally aimed only at the occupation of the coasts of Holland and Belgium, as a means of forcing England to end the war. The success momentarily unnerved Hitler, he did not realise that France was in collapse and that the southern flank of the penetration was safe.

Now that he was there, he hardly knew what to do about it. No preparations at all had been made for a cross-Channel attack; the means were not there, the Navy to cover them was not there. There was only the Luftwaffe, which over Dunkirk especially had already had a taste of the R.A.F.

Dunkirk was no miracle: the British got away because the Germans were not powerful enough to stop them. But to the German troops, as they made their way through the burning streets, wary of toppling buildings and the whine of snipers' bullets, it seemed that 'Old Adolf' had worked his usual miracle. Here was all the chaos of retreat – wrecked 3-ton lorries on the promenade, abandoned guns and all the strange, incongruous litter of war, the sunken ships in the harbour and off the beaches, the thousands of steel helmets making crazy patterns on the sand dunes, the dirty, dusty, unshaven prisoners wearing the stunned small-boy look of recent captivity.

They had smashed through to the Channel coast in three weeks, had been part of the armoured columns moving resistlessly and in overwhelming power through a stunned, sullen and blazing countryside. They felt like Gods.

A few weeks later the staff car of Field Marshal Kesselring, commander of Air Fleet 2, came whining down the dusty, poplar-lined roads of the Pas de Calais. Here and there it stopped, the Field Marshal got out, followed by his staff, alert with map-boards and binoculars.

For his own command post, he chose a site on the great, gaunt headland of Cap Gris-Nez, that juts out towards England from between Calais and Boulogne, the nearest part of the continent to the defiant and still fighting island.

After him came the Labour Service battalions – the German Pioneer Corps – and ground administrative units, the signals units, and the airfield flak artillery of Lieutenant-General Dessloch, an old cavalryman and airman. The corn went down, beaten flat; trees on the boundaries fell under the axes of the Labour Service men, stripped to the waist. Vehicles bumped over the ruined fields, signal wires were run out, telephones installed and tested. Lorries groaned along the roads from Germany, bringing bombs, petrol, ammunition, the ten thousand and one spares that an air force or an army needs.

When the men paused in their work, they could see, out across the Channel, the English ships passing under the white cliffs in monstrous convoys, between twenty and thirty ships at a time.

The sea gleamed silver in the sunshine, gay and inviting under the summer sun.

The first planes came in, Junkers 87s, circling the new airfields, throttling back, and as they lowered their flaps, sinking onto the ground and running to a standstill in clouds of dust. Then the fighters, the Me 109s and 110s of General Osterkamp's Wing. And the Heinkels of Coeler's IX Group, recently – very recently – trained in minelaying. And the Junkers 88s of the crack squadrons which had attacked Scapa Flow and the Firth of Forth – the Eagle Squadron – the trained ship-destroyers.

They were accustomed to victory, they swept forward with the smoke of battle. They had led the advance into Holland, had flown and fed the fires of blazing Rotterdam. The Ju 88s of the Eagle Squadron had destroyed the aerodromes and flak defences of Rotterdam, the Hague and Delft. The long-range bombers had set the city on fire behind the defenders, as they surrendered, and Holland had capitulated next day. It was called an atrocity then, but it was merely the first of a long series which was to include Cassino, Caen and Cleve. They had turned and led the panzers to Dunkirk; and met the R.A.F. high above the beaches; and had there suffered their most severe losses. For all their skill and courage, they had not been able to prevent the evacuation. And there were new faces in the mess, new pilots and aircrews from the training schools, as well as the old hands, some of whom could remember the harsh mountains of Spain and the practical lessons they had learned there against the Russian Ratas.

Every night now, there were briefings for the minelayers of IX Group. Searchlights, cutting a tunnel of light through the darkness for a moment, the heavily-laden aircraft lumbering forward. Blind take-off, mainly on instruments; the aircraft barely clearing the hedge, then airborne at last and lumbering up into the night sky. Set course for Dover, Thames, Portsmouth, Plymouth, Portland. Still new to the job, and a vivid flash below the aircraft. Hell! misjudged it. That one must have drifted on to the land, or on to the rocks down there.

The sea, like a black carpet, speckled with moonlight; and the flak that comes up at you slowly, and then suddenly seems to increase speed as it whistles by. The land, much darker than the sea, but more vague, with no moon reflection and no lights at all, except the little winking fireflies of the guns. Woof! The aircraft rocks. Last mine gone now what's the course for home?

The Germans knew, and none better than Hitler, that the British Empire was not Belgium; they could not blow it down – nevertheless, they tried to puff it down. From every radio station in 'Great Germany', and relayed to the Armed Forces occupying the conquered nations of Europe, came the most-plugged tune of the period: 'Bomben auf En-ge-land'. The lyric, describing the bombers soaring like eagles over their prey, was mixed with the recorded, swelling roar of aero engines and punctuated by the boom of a big drum, as in the more famous 'Wir fahren gegen En-ge-land', which had earned for a certain composer the honorary title of 'Herr Professor Boom-Boom'. The bomber pilots loved 'Bomben auf En-ge-land' as much as the British soldiers did comparative ditties, like 'Run, Rabbit, Run' and 'The Washing'. That is, it made them sick.

It was too obviously written by a parlour-patriot in an ill-spent five minutes for pecuniary gain. The only recording which really caught on, and that was much later, was 'Lili Marlen' sung by Laia Andersen.

There were many other similarities. In the R.A.F. the automatic pilot was 'George'; in the Luftwaffe it was 'Emil'. (In the U.S.A.A.F. it was 'Iron Mike'.) The Station Warrant Officer's patter for aircraftsmen was: 'Thought? Whatdermean – you thought? You're not paid to think.' An Oberfeldwebel's line was: 'Leave it to the horses, they've got bigger heads.' Mess etiquette in the Luftwaffe was more formal – but the bows and heel-clicks had to be just right, just sufficiently casual, like the difference between 'How d'you do?' and 'Pleased to meet you', or you were damned, in spite of Hitler's social levelling. The only major difference was that, at table, one German hand rests on the table, the other on the lap; the English put both on the lap.

Bedrooms were more likely to contain pin-ups than pictures of the Fuhrer. In fact, the two nations were extraordinarily alike; and they both agreed that there was, in fact, a Master Race; the only difference of opinion, and that slight, was as to which one of them it was; and this was now to be fought out.

Field Marshal Kesselring was confident. From his command post on Cap Gris-Nez the Channel convoys passed, so to speak, under his window. He could see, directly, the operations of Group Captain Fink's 2nd Bomber Wing; and the battle fought by General Osterkamp's 1st Fighter Wing. Reports came in of the successes further afield of Air Groups VIII and IX against shipping in the Channel, off the east coast, and in harbour. He saw the convoys pass and the bombers plunge at them, while the fighters held the R.A.F. in check; he saw the gaps torn in the long lines as sinking colliers turned away, wreathed in smoke, foundering under his eyes. The battle, he thought, went well. The merchantmen were being murdered, there was no sign of the Royal Navy, little of their air force. The barrier to invasion was being broken down.

One thing he did not see, which his airmen did not notice, was the behaviour of the masters of the coasters and their engine-room staff. No ship sank in the swept channel unless she was actually blown to bits or thrown out of control. The ships went ashore to die. Hit and burning, listing over in the water, with the sea pouring in, the colliers drove towards the land, sinking even as they steamed ahead. The unwritten rule of the road was that no ship must sink in the fairway and block the channel for other ships. And with stubborn pride and courage they obeyed.

By the end of the first week of August, all Kesselring's airfields were ready and the main forces of Air Fleet 2 moved in, including Air Groups I and IV, the latter being strategic bombers, and the C.A.I. – the Italian contingent.

In that month, the Italians wandered over to Dover; and were then directed to try for Channel convoys as they passed Margate at dusk. They did not add to the 'paling fence' of sunken ships at the side of the fairway. Indeed, as a collier master put it, 'We hoped they'd get the job permanent.'

They were not, in fact, particularly lacking in courage, but their aircraft and their technique left something to be desired. The Germans were a different matter; and they were by now very experienced.

As the bombers go, they can look down at Cap Gris-Nez below. Some squadrons now take care to rendezvous with the fighters well to one side or the other of Cap Gris-Nez, so that there will be no chance of an irate R/T recall from the Field Marshal's command post.

They flew west, climbing. The sea fell away, a sheet of many-coloured glass, scored by frozen waves; not the waves a sailor knows, for they had no height when seen from above, they were merely long wedge-shaped patterns permanently scarred on the water, motionless, like tadpoles, and getting smaller. The sea was very dark in places, not from clustered seaweed, but cloud shadow; and away to starboard it broke in a white line against the shores of the moated island.

And over there a huddle of ships going down Channel, flying balloons; small ships, but many of them, more than twenty. Still coming.

But today they were not the target. In each of the Ju 88s, the front gunner, sitting on the right of the pilot, had switched on the dive-bomb sights; the red light glowed. He reported: 'All clear.' The rear formations were still in 'Vs' but the leader's section was going into line-astern already. They went in directly over the Isle of Wight, changing into their attack formation with the speed and ease of long practice.

It had been like this at Scapa Flow, on the first operational flight of a crack squadron, newly equipped with the Junkers 88 – the 'Wonder Bomber'. Rearing columns of water alongside the battleship *Iron Duke* – only a training ship, out of commission, but still, a battleship. The British had had to beach her in Longhope Sound – and admitted the loss of a rabbit.

Then Norway. British warships again, and this time without the flak protection of a fleet anchorage. Even so, the smoke of the shell-bursts had looked like a carpet suspended in mid-air. After that – Holland. Only two months ago. Now, here was the Isle of Wight, with the Needles Channel to port – and on the southern side, the 'Needles Graveyard', with masts and funnels and half-submerged hulls lying in the surf, the place where bombed and mined ships went to die, limping out of the convoy lines by day and night.

Away to starboard was another squadron of Ju 88s, also going into attack formation, as the coast-line leapt towards them.

The two squadrons crossed the coast, out of the sun, at over 300 m.p.h. and attacked with blinding speed; the guns began to

61

fire only as the leaders started to dive. They came down almost vertically, from 10,000 feet.

Above the pilot's head, a number of red lines were painted on the perspex; as he pushed the stick forward and the nose sank down, the horizon rose up to the first red line – 40 degrees of dive. Then 50, 60, 70. Degrees of dive, like degrees of bank, always seem steeper than they are; and this was the simple check. Beside the pilot, the front gunner had cocked his gun, his finger was curled round the trigger, ready to blaze away as they came near the ground.

The pilot was looking straight down, now, at the target. He could see the hangars through the dive-bomb sight – a parallelo-gram of wire enclosed the aerodrome; and the aerodrome seemed to be growing in size all the time, growing outside the bomb-sight. The pilot steered gently, to take in a particular hangar, as that in turn came up at him, expanding as it came. To the pilot, it did not seem that he was moving; merely that the aerodrome was getting bigger, blown up in a few seconds from a pocket-handkerchief to a size where individual aircraft, parked round the perimeter, became clear, and men – yes, men, running, or simply standing, looking upwards, the white blur of their faces perfectly distinct. But the pilot was not thinking of them, he was thinking of the wind; it was drifting him slightly so that the hangar began to slip away from the bomb-sight, under him. He pushed the stick forward a trifle, and increased the angle of dive: now, he was almost vertical.

He was falling out of the sun, and the sun was high; the perspex canopy was lit up by the sun, the cockpit was in shadow. There was very little noise. To the men below, the diving bomber seemed to come down like an express train, screaming like all the fiends in hell. The dive-brakes which in normal flight lay flat underneath the wings were now extended; like Venetian blinds in appearance, they obstructed the passage of the air past the machine, and the air screamed in fury. They held the bomber steady in its plunge, prevented the speed from rising above a certain safe figure, kept the aircraft comfortably plummetting down, so that it could come right down to the deck and still pull out.

But the pilot heard nothing of this, only a distant howling scream. He had a helmet on, earphones tight; oxygen mask over his mouth, and a microphone; he was conscious of a whisper only of the gale of sound that accompanied his split-second plunge from the heights. As the pilot pressed the button of the bomb release, the gunner fired, raking the running figures on the ground, the sand-bagged Lewis gun emplacement.

The machine had already started to pull out, before the bombs had even been released, for in that way only would they follow the line of flight and hit the target. And as the bombs fell away the pilot felt a backward pressure on the control column – an 'automatic pull-out' device had come into operation, trimming down the tail to help him flatten out in time. Even so, the big twin-motor bomber came very close to the ground, pulling out 50 feet above the trees on the aerodrome boundary and seeming to bounce back into the sky, almost grazing the hangar roof.

Below it, one corner of the hangar roof took off, separated from the rest, and went cartwheeling through the air; smoke and flame came bursting out of the hangar, and it seemed to sag in the middle. But the Ju 88 was away, all gunners ripping off long bursts at the ground to cover their escape, for this was the most dangerous point of the whole performance. For a few breathless moments, the pilot had to fly steadily, straight ahead and climbing slightly, as he pulled up the dive-breaks. Some pilots preferred to go right down on the deck to do this, when the flak was heavy; but few people had the nerve – or the knowledge – to let a dive-bomber put in its attack first, and then shoot it down when it was a sitting bird.

There was a sudden yell from the gunner, and his gun stopped firing. 'Verdammte Scheisse!' Just the right moment to have a gun jam. But behind him, the other bombers of the squadron were plunging down into the smoke of the already burning aerodrome; there was a long line of them, coming down and looking like a ladder standing up in the sky. Nose to tail, at three second intervals, they fell towards the inferno, adding to the chaos. Both hangars were on fire, the girders fallen onto the trapped aeroplanes within. The wing of an aeroplane was blown, fluttering, across the grass like a piece of paper. Other aeroplanes, around the perimeter, were fluffing up in flames and slowly collapsing in sparks and smoke. One aeroplane rose into the air, vertically, like a helicopter and came down on top of another. Clods of earth rained down upon the wreckage, as fresh bombs exploded. Then it was all over. The Ju 88s had gone, and one of their escort, diving casually in farewell, fired a balloon.

The balloon left a black smear down the sky, burning halfway down to the ground. The attack had taken three minutes.

The Junkers 87 so imprinted itself on the minds of its enemies

63

that it still carries its class-label as a personal, particular name. It was one of many different types of stuka, from the original Curtiss 'Helldiver', through the Henschel 123, to the twin-motor Junkers 88. But to the men who sailed in the convoys, 'Stuka' means the Junkers 87 and nothing else. It was the plane that deprived them of their grub and grog, perversely attacking at noon or shortly after. They liked resentfully to believe that that was why many of the stuka attacks came at mid-day.

They came when they could at that hour because, flying out of the south, they had the sun high and behind; they came down on the ships, unseen until the last moment, and when seen, hard to make out and harder still to hit. Few people ever saw a Ju 88 squadron go into line astern – they came too fast. But the Ju 87 was a different proposition. The visual difference was that the Ju 88 was a big twin-engined bomber, with a crew of four crammed tightly in the nose; the Ju 87 was single-engined, with a pilot and rear gunner under a raised canopy, and a fixed undercarriage – the extreme dihedral angle of the wings made them appear, from some angles, to be swept forward.

For the toad beneath the harrow, the difference was that the Ju 88 carried four 550-lb. bombs externally under the wings and sixteen 110-lb. bombs (or an extra fuel tank) in the fuselage; the Ju 87 brought them a single 1,100-lb. bomb under the fuselage (swung clear by two arms, when released, so that it cleared the airscrew), and four 110-lb. bombs externally under the wings.

For the aircrews, the difference was that the Ju 88 was an extremely fast 'evader' bomber capable of well over 300 m.p.h.; it could nip over to the English coast, cripple a convoy or smash an aerodrome, and be halfway back to France before the British fighters even reached the smoke plumes from the blazing target. But it was poorly-armed and could not fight.

The Ju 87 was much slower – it could neither fight nor run. It was tied to the Army – part of what we would now call the Tactical Air Force – and could operate only under fighter cover or against countries whose air force had already been beaten down. It was the main weapon used against the convoys in the opening phases of the battle but, up against first-class fighter opposition for the first time, lost heavily and was eventually withdrawn. It had one last kick in November 1940, against targets in the Thames Estuary, and then never saw England again – in daylight. But it was used for occasional 'moonlight stalking' attacks on Channel convoys during 1941.

The dive-bomber, though more widely used by the Germans

than by anyone else, was not German – it was American. Some of the group of old 1914-1918 war pilots who planned and controlled the re-birth of the German air force visited the United States, and brought back with them this conception of a small, handy, easily-produced bomber, which was accurate enough to knock out a tank, or pillbox; very useful for the new Wehrmacht.

In the end, it was out-dated – except on the Russian front against an antique air force; its function was taken over by the rocket-armed fighter-bombers of the Allies – equally deadly, and very much faster. Against convoys a new technique – of torpedo plus bomb – was also evolved by the Allies, painfully and slowly. But, in its day, for all its limitations, the stuka was just as effective – as the bottom of the English Channel indicates.

9 · Coal From Newcastle

AT Phoenix Wharf, Southampton, the day began just like any other day. George Reid, the wharf foreman, was superintending the discharging of a collier, never an easy job at any time. Time is money to ship-owners, they like a quick turn-round, and that means that the wharf men, organised in their different teams, must work with a blaze of speed; and work in with each other. Now, it was even more important that they should free the ship of her cargo and send her away.

She had to join a convoy which would form up at the Mother-bank, 'light', later that day for the long trip back to the coal ports of the east coast. Colliers discharging at Dover or Shoreham were no trouble to their wharves – they had all day. To be precise, they had several days. They were what the Naval Control Service called 'joiners' – they would come out to rejoin the convoy as it passed them on the way back. The ships which discharged at Southampton would arrive there long after the 'joiners' were snug in Dover, Newhaven and Shoreham, and they would have to leave long before the others did. Every minute counted. If the ship was not completely empty when her sailing time came, she would sail all the same – taking some of her coal back to Newcastle.

So the different teams which made up the wharf labour force were putting their backs into it. At any moment, a raid or an alarm might stop all work for an unknown period – and a ship that had come through the hazards of the east coast and Channel to bring coal for the homes and industry of the south might have wasted her journey or be kept hanging about, empty, for a week. Then the sirens wailed over the River Itchen and out across Southampton Water. The crane drivers came scrambling down from their cabs, it was dangerous to be caught by bombs up there, perched fifty feet above the docks. The trimmers in the hold of the ship carried on for a few minutes. The drivers of the locomotives stopped their engines and got out – if the cranes packed up, they had better pack up. The men on the bagging platforms under the big hoppers kept on filling the sacks with

66

coal and man-handling them onto the row of Army lorries that were loading there. In the office, the clerks looked up; the girl telephonist plugged in a number. Mr S. W. Dennett, a Director of the company, glanced up from his desk. Another alarm. There had been hundreds of them, and rarely did they mean anything.

On the deck of the collier the men were running to their guns. The 12-pdr on the stern elevated and trained round; the Lewis gun on 'Monkey Island' was manned. The spotter on the wharf, always the last under cover, signalled: 'This is it. Take cover.' There was a thin, high drumming rumble, increasing in volume, coming straight up Southampton Water. A lorry driver dived straight into the dirt underneath his lorry. The office staff crawled under their desks. Half a dozen men, caught far from the shelter, swarmed over the wharf and into a small space underneath.

Directly opposite them, on the other side of the Itchen, was priority one target – two large factories of Vickers-Supermarine, making Spitfires. Alongside them was the Southampton gasworks.

It was the 26th September, 1940. Everyone was slightly jumpy, the Germans had been trying repeatedly for Vickers-Supermarine over the river – and what the Germans attempted, they did, even if they had to make two or three attacks. Dead and dying men were still being dug out of the shelters there, after an attack three days before by two dozen Jabos – Me 109 fighter-bombers. The skyline opposite was bare and splintered from the bombs dropped eleven days before by two squadrons of Dorniers, which had ripped down in a shallow-dive attack to 2,000 feet and then picked up their formation again with breathless speed and ease, a prima donna performance. The bomb-aiming had been less perfect, and Vickers-Supermarine still stood. Everyone knew that it was being evacuated; everyone knew that the Germans knew the place intimately, for German pilots had visited it before the war. Their crack liners *Bremen* and *Europa* carried a Walrus – the 'Steam Pigeon' – built at those works, and the pilots came to collect them from the factory.

A collier lay alongside Phoenix Wharf, one of the 'regulars'. She was the *Tamworth*, the 'Unsinkable Ship', and she still bore the scars of her mauling off Dover two months before; her master was still Charles Logan Sclanders, her 12-pdr gunlayer was still John Gallagher, now with the B.E.M. About this time Eric Speakman, the Naval rating manning the Lewis, had left her to join another ship doing the same run. The two ships were abeam, opposite each other in the two divisions of the convoy off Beachy Head, when Speakman's new ship was hit; they saw her go down with all hands. But that was the only way the ships and the men could be stopped – by sinking them.

The grabs were out, discharging her. The cranes rattled round from the hold to the hoppers and back again; the grabs came plunging into the hold, to settle in the coal; cables tightened, and the teeth of the grabs closed upon the coal, then swung up and out, clear of the ship, and round to the mouths of the hopper. They hung there, a moment, then opened; there was a puff in the air like smoke, which was coal dust, as the loads thundered into the hoppers; and the coal dust blew away over the dusty wharf. The trimmers in the hold of the ship had already stepped forward again, with their shovels and rakes, to prepare the coal for the next drop of the grabs.

Along the quay grunted a small locomotive, a long line of wagons clattering and banging after it; it puffed along angrily for a few yards, then stopped. A chute, leading down from a hopper, was directly over the first wagon; a man, standing high up near the top of the hopper and dressed in the oldest of old clothes, pulled a lever – and a shower of coal from Northumberland or the East Midlands went thundering down the chute into the wagon. With another movement of the lever, he checked the fall of coal, and the engine grunted forward a few more yards, with a thumping and banging of buffers, until the next wagon was under the chute.

On the other side a row of Army lorries were feeding from a hopper – some of it was bulk, and some of it was bagged. The men on the bagging platform filled their sacks from small chutes, then they were man-handled over the tail-boards. Other men were operating the grading plant – gigantic sieves, high in the air, incorporated in the hoppers, over which the coal jumped and bounced as the screen of the sieves vibrated. There was continual noise, and hard, high-speed accurate work. The siren sounded, wailing over the Itchen River and out across Southampton Water. In the office, the clerks looked up for a moment from their ledgers; the girl telephonist plugged in a number, not even glancing up. Mr Dennett, the Director responsible for the wharf, wondered how many hours he would lose. Probably only another reconnaissance plane.

The crane-drivers came swarming down fifty feet from their cabs, down the bare, vertical ladders that led to the ground and safety. The cranes were still – like necks of enormous storks they leaned out over the *Tamworth*. The grunting locomotive came to an angry stop. The men on the bagging platforms looked up, then carried on for a moment. There was a high drumming rumble, increasing in volume, coming straight up Southampton Water. The driver of one of the lorries which was waiting to load from a hopper, flung himself under the chassis. Men caught near the quayside, far from the shelter, swarmed over the edge of the wharf and underneath it. Men pounded along the steel decks of the collier towards the guns. The clerks crawled under their desks. The spotter, always last under cover, signalled: 'This is it. Take cover.' The last laggards dived for it.

The sky above the Itchen looked like an aerial parade at a Nuremberg Rally. In stately formation, sailing disdainfully through the shell bursts, came fifty bombers. Over them a furious fighter dogfight was taking place, but the bombers came on with contemptuous ease; none of the fighters got near the bombers, the Me 109s brushed them aside, harried them, engaged them in a chaos of diving, curving rocketting machines. The air was suddenly alive with the rising whine of falling bombs, a protest of the air that seemed to pitch up suddenly into an unbearable scream and burst in a great, rumbling series of explosions.

The Vickers-Supermarine works, on the opposite side of the river, seemed – a witness said – 'to burn up like a piece of brown paper', a bit of brown paper to which a match has been set, curling up from the bottom and then collapsing upon itself in charred fragments. It was, he said, 'Precision bombing – and damn good bombing.' A burning man fell towards the river from 20,000 feet, his parachute dissolving in a wisp and trail of smoke, faint against the sky. He fell towards the surface with frightful force – there was a splash, and he was gone.

The far side of the river disappeared under gigantic, rolling clouds of smoke and dust. There would be no more Spitfires built at Southampton. The cloud went on pouring up, as though feeding on itself, and rose and drifted and smeared the sky down as far as Calshot. Dazed, the men and women on the wharf came out of their hiding places and watched it. There was a grim, approaching rumble from the west, drifting away from the heights; the spotter, last under cover, signalled: 'This is it. Take cover.' This time it was.

The office staff got under their desks, the office boy dived for the accumulator pit, a driver and his mate got beneath their lorry. The driver who had previously taken cover under his lorry now ran for the edge of the wharf, where the little party there were again disappearing. It looked safer, there was concrete overhead as protection. The spotter, as usual, was last under cover – this time he beat by a short head an eight-ton railway wagon which was somersaulting through the air.

In ten seconds a hundred and fifty bombs burst on the wharf, on the gasworks alongside, or in the river. The surface of the water simply rose up above the decks of the collier, lying by the quay, with her 12-pdr cracking away and adding to the din. Hoppers, grading plant, briquette works, engine room, weighbridge, offices were gouged, wrecked or blotted out, the Army lorries loading at the bagging platform reduced to scrap metal. The men and women huddled in the shelter, close together, felt the structure not trembling but vibrating, as if it were a mouse which a cat had got by the neck and was shaking. A frightful, elemental force raged over the wharf, and battered the breath out of their bodies. Then it stopped. As they staggered out into the sunlight, expecting to see they knew not what, they found a dim world of dust and smoke – and the whole surface of the wharf seemed to have changed colour and to be moving. It was liquid, and it lapped over their shoes.

It was hot tar from the gasworks, over which lay the silence of death. It was a ruin, breathing out dust and smoke. From this side of the river, too, clouds of it funnelled up from the rubble and began to drift away to Calshot and the Channel. Above it, high above it, the last thirty bombers of the day were flying home. They streamed southwards, in diamond formations of four, disdainfully through the gun smoke, with the whirling condensation trails of their escort writing half-circles in the sky, beating off the British fighters which were trying to get at them. None did.

A policeman came out of the smoke towards the party in the shelter. The raid was not over yet, as far as they knew, and what he asked them for was a volunteer to send a message from the telephone exchange. The girl telephonist volunteered at once, walking calmly off with him as though there was no danger and never had been. The office was wrecked, but the telephone exchange was still in working order. The policeman asked her to put through a call to the A.R.P.; when she got them, he gave her the message to pass: that there was an unexploded bomb – underneath the telephone exchange at Phoenix Wharf. The girl never turned a hair, and calmly transmitted the message. She was later awarded the O.B.E.

All over the wharf, men were sorting themselves out. Those who had been in the shelter, found that it had been straddled by three bombs. No one was hurt. The two men who had crawled under their lorry, staggered out, shocked and deafened – the front of the lorry had been shattered and crumpled in by a bomb which had landed two yards away. The office boy climbed out of the accumulator pit. One of the six men hiding under the wharf had been blown off it, into the mud, and injured. One man did not move. He was the driver who had first hid under his lorry, and then thought it not safe enough. It was not – a steel cylinder had struck it from above, going right down through the driver's cab. It had had his name on it, and he had escaped it; but he had not escaped, he lay quite silent under the wharf, where a heavy piece of concrete had been blown through, pulping his skull so that he had no head at all. When they tried to move him, he simply fell to pieces.

When men climbed up on the hoppers, to investigate the extent of the damage, they found a bath among the coal, and taps and bits of porcelain. These came from hundreds of yards away, from a works making bathroom equipment and fittings; it was now collapsed, just a heap of bricks, slates and woodwork. Many hours after it was all over, and all the casualties cleared to hospital or the mortuary, an old woman came crawling out of the wreckage, dusty, dirty and furious. She was the caretaker.

The wharf was totally out of action, all the machinery wrecked and the hoppers damaged, but the casualties were very light; in the gasworks it was another story. After George Lewis, the wharf's first-aid man, had attended to their own people, he hurried over there. Nearly twenty of the men had been hiding in a marine boiler, they had been buried by coal and none came out unhurt. There were many dead and many wounded, many blast casualties lying silent and white, like dusty bundles of old rags. There was very little blood, for their injuries were mainly internal and blast had closed the surface wounds. For many hours, what remained of the wharf's transport was taking them to hospital. No ambulances had arrived, and the tyres of the cars and lorries were in most cases punctured. For the moment, the work of mercy took precedence over coal.

Outside the Civic Centre, the casualty lists started to go up. Many of the bodies were unidentified, and unidentifiable. A descriptive note, to help recognition of one unknown corpse,

71

read simply: 'Teeth, not false.' There were curses among the little groups of people standing by the notice board. But there was no feeling of terror, most people were in good spirits, if a bit sobered.

There was really no need for soldierly exortations from far-distant politicians. Though they continued to pour forth, from utterly surprising sources, the seaport of Southampton carried on; the work of the battered coal wharves was transferred to other docks, at some cost in efficiency, and the colliers kept on coming.

In fact, the Battle of Britain was nearing its end and a new phase of the war about to open – the Blockade of Britain, with the emphasis once more upon the destruction of the convoys. Invasion had been indefinitely postponed; it was clear, even to junior German infantry officers, as the clumsy river barges wallowed in the surf off the Dutch coast, that if this was what happened in an exercise, then invasion, as an Operation, 'was simply not on'. The Luftwaffe was left, for a month or so, to fast-bowl the batsman on its own, with the fielders and the wicket-keeper gone to tea.

They bowled well; the coastal aerodromes had been chewed up, the sector stations brought for a time near to disintegration, the aircraft factories near the coast badly savaged. At Southampton alone, Vickers-Supermarine had gone and before that the Cunliffe-Owen works at Eastleigh, where eight dive-bombers caught a shift at work and there were heavy casualties. The sheds of that factory now lay, like burnt-out Zeppelins, on the grass. The bombers had suffered painful loss on the approaches to London, though virtually nowhere else; but Luftwaffe operational strength had been reduced only by about one-third. However, there was no future for them in daylight operations, as the bombers could not operate by day beyond the range of their fighter escort – which meant that they could reach London, but could not penetrate beyond, unless Göring was prepared to lose half of them. All of Great Britain beyond that line was safe from them by day; and day by day the factories and shipyards in that part of the country free of them – about nine-tenths of the island – were turning out the means of defence and the cause of their eventual destruction.

So they turned to night bombing, against which Fighter Command was ill-prepared; and the bombers went by darkness to the targets they dared not attempt in the daylight; and they tried to strangle the island by smashing the great ports and the shipping which came into them. They used many new weapons and techniques and, as the autumn gave way to winter the waters of the Thames Estuary suddenly erupted with a new menace.

10 · *E-Boat Alley*

CAPTAIN POTTS, of the *Betswood*, stirred restless in his sleep. Blinking, and vaguely uneasy, he glanced out of the port-hole. What he saw there sent him out of his bunk and running in desperate haste for the bridge ladder. He had seen a ship, with the seas breaking over her.

The officer on duty looked round in surprise at the sudden appearance of the master. Potts rapped out:

'Full astern: Hard-a-starboard.'

The telegraphs rang, and the wheel went over, the *Betswood* stopping, then going astern and turning, regardless of any confusion to the other ships of convoy F.S. 69, then steaming down the Norfolk coast for London. His desperate action saved the ship, but other masters were not so wide awake; they blindly followed their leaders.

Within a short time there were six merchantmen and an armed trawler of the escort lying stopped, with heavy seas breaking violently over them and rapidly pounding them to pieces. It was this sight, of waves breaking broadside over a ship, which had warned the master of the *Betswood*. It means only one thing – the ship is aground; and in this area that meant one other thing – the Haisborough Sands, which form the northern entrance to E-boat alley.

There were 171 men in the stranded ships. Nothing could save the ships, they were disintegrating underneath their crews minute by minute; but it might still be possible to save the men. The roar of the waves pounding on that strip of half-submerged sand, lying in a great arc round the curve of the Norfolk coast, was sufficient warning of the peril into which their boats must go.

To this pass they had come, by blindly playing follow-my-leader, not bothering to do their own navigation, as a check, just in case. One after the other, like the mythical soldiers who marched over a cliff on parade formation because no one said 'Halt!' they had driven in succession upon the foam-covered sands. And now, in this August gale of 1941, they must soon drown, unless rescue came.

It did come, in the shape of the two Cromer lifeboats under Coxswain Blogg, G.C., and the efforts of the surviving ships of the convoy. But for thirty-seven of them rescue was too late or utterly impossible by reason of the height and fury of the seas, and they drowned that night upon the Haisborough.

In the whole of 1941, 268 ships were sunk or wrecked, not by the enemy, but by the perils of the sea. They totalled 418,164 tons. It was inevitable, for the ships were unnaturally massed and marshalled together, passing at night down narrow treacherous channels where, at first, all navigational signs had been removed. Later, very dim lights, shaded from above, were shown by the buoys – but in a night of driving rain or howling storm, with the vessels shipping it green and spray bursting like hail continually over the bridge, it was not hard to make a fatal error. To these hazards, the perils of the enemy were only additional; though they were serious enough.

On 26th November, 1940, two months to the day after she had lain alongside Phoenix Wharf as it was swept by the bombs, the *Tamworth* steamed slowly up the Itchen and again came alongside – the first ship to be discharged there after the bombing as she had been the last before it. The grabs swung out and began to discharge her, and all was as it had been. No single blows could cripple the island – only a sustained, throttling pressure on the ports and sea routes. This the Germans now set out to apply.

They were well situated to do it, for they held the Low Countries and Northern France. Since the time of the first Elizabeth, Englishmen had gone to fight and die there; to deny that area to a potential enemy had been the first aim of British policy for centuries. It was a dagger pointed at the mouth of the Thames. Though the Germans increased the scale of their attacks against the western lifelines in the Atlantic, at first by U-boats and raiders and then increasingly with long-range bombers, the main weight of their attack throughout 1940 fell in the area of the Nore Command.

The centre of gravity of that Command was the Thames Estuary – the focal point of the east coast and Channel convoys, the great assembly and dispersal area of the ships. Its right wing was the 'hot spot' of Dover Straits, where England comes nearest to France; its left wing was the Essex and Norfolk coast, where England comes nearest to Holland, and that was the 'hot spot' of E-boat Alley. In the Dutch Naval bases of Den Helder and Ijmuiden, the Germans built up a striking force of E-boats to harry the east coast convoys at the point nearest to them; in Northern France and the Low Countries they had already Kesselring's Luftflotte 2, with its specially-trained anti-shipping Air Group IX.

The E-boats used the mine and the torpedo; the aircraft used the mine, the torpedo, and the bomb. It was the mines which claimed the most, and most of them were laid in the area of the Nore Command. One hundred and sixteen ships (355,776 tons) were sunk by mines in this small area during 1940, whereas the loss by mine of all the other commands put together was only 85 ships. As minelayers, the aircraft and the E-boats were complementary; for the bombers laid their mines where the E-boats could not penetrate – inside the estuaries; and both together, sometimes aided by destroyers, mined the swept channels outside.

By daylight air action they increased the difficulty of re-opening the mined channels and making safe the estuaries; they attacked the minesweepers so incessantly that, in August 1940, the decision was taken to discontinue day sweeping and carry it out at night, a much more difficult and costly process. In this way, all their efforts led towards one goal – and the Battle of the Blockade had begun.

August 1940 was the month of decision. In that month, the Channel convoys ran the Straits by night instead of by day; the A.A. Guard, the Mobile Balloon Barrage Flotilla, the 'Maritime A.A.' were formed; the *Hunt*-class destroyers, with their heavy A.A. armament took over escort duty in the Channel; the minesweepers turned to work by night instead of by day; the Admiralty codes and ciphers, broken by the Germans, were changed; and the number of ships in the Channel convoys was reduced. So that, while the Battle of Britain was only just beginning and invasion was a possibility, the Admiralty had laid already the framework on which they would fight the Battle of the Blockade.

And in August the Germans struck twice with new weapons. On the 23rd Naval aircraft of the IX Air Group attacked with torpedoes a convoy in the Moray Firth, sinking two ships and damaging a third. It was an impressive debut for the German airborne torpedo, and the threat seemed serious; but, as they possessed only about two dozen of these specialised aircraft, no large or sustained attacks were possible. On the 25th the Admiralty issued a warning that there had been recently a number of mysterious explosions near ships, and that the cause was prob-

ably a new type of mine, working on the acoustic principle
and fired by the sound waves caused by the movement of ships
through the water.

In September, one of these mines was dropped on land, by
error, and the theory was confirmed. In that month also, the
E-boats moved to their Dutch bases and began to strike at the
east coast convoys off Sheringham with a force which varied
between ten and fifteen boats; and German destroyers ventured
once across to the west coast to lay a big minefield off Falmouth.
It contained new booby-traps, known as explosive sweep-
cutters, which make sweeping a much more difficult business.
No E-boat was sunk until October, when Nore Command
destroyers nailed one of these elusive mosquitoes. But the
E-boats sank 23 ships (47,986 tons) during the year. Then, the
Germans introduced a delay-action device into the magnetic
mine, so that it would lie on the bottom without reacting at all
to the sweepers passing it; the area would be declared free of
mines – and days later would come the shock.

Captain Sclanders of the *Tamworth* experienced this, on his
way into the Thames, but, like Potts of the *Betswood*, he seemed
unsinkable. The *Tamworth* was queuing to get through the
'Gate', with one small 400-ton ship ahead of her and a big
14,000 tonner abeam. The pilot of the big fellow hailed him to
go first, which he did. As he went through, it followed. There
was a flash and a spurt of water, then the roar of the exploding
mine, and the 14,000 tonner started to settle down. There was
another roar ahead, and as Captain Sclanders looked round, he
saw the last of the small ship, as she disappeared under the
water. Some of her crew had just had time to jump for it, and
they were simming around in the wreckage; but before he could
lower a boat, a motor launch came out to them.

Scenes like these were repeated many times in the Thames
Estuary. On one night – 12th/13th December, 1940 – at least
fifty magnetic mines were laid between Southend and the Isle
of Sheppey; they were fitted with a $4\frac{1}{2}$-day delayed action fuse,
and became 'live' simultaneously. That day, seven ships were
sunk. And from then on, for more than two weeks, ships were
stumbling over others and sending them up. By laying magnetic
mines, delayed-action magnetic mines, and acoustic mines all in
the same area, the Germans could and did produce a 'marmalade'
of unpleasantness difficult to sweep and nerve-wracking to sail
over. Some masters hardly dared go astern, even in emergency,
for fear the sound would put up an acoustic mine under them.

All this, and a good deal more elsewhere, was produced by a small force of about eighty night-bombers whose losses were negligible. It was a very paying proposition indeed, as the R.A.F. discovered, too, but boring for the crews who rarely or never saw the certain results of their labour, though they saw it in general – the steady growth of that 'paling fence' of masts and funnels sticking out of estuaries and beside the swept channels, to which the bombers and the E-boats also contributed.

To begin with, the only defence against these attacks was the odd patrol boat, armed only with machine-guns. The mine-layers had to fly low, and some did fall victim in this way. Early in 1941, construction work began in the Thames on a vast project to raise great sea towers on stilts across the estuary and off Harwich. These were the Maunsell Forts, referred to in Chapter 4.

Each Fort was actually a complex of towers, holding a useful selection of heavy and medium-range A.A. guns, together with radar and searchlights. The artillery included four 3.7-inch guns and two 40-mm Bofors. Three of the Thames Estuary forts were Army-manned – the romantically named Great Nore Tower, Red Sand Tower and Shivering Sand Tower; two were Navy-manned – Tongue Sand Tower and Knock John Tower; and, in addition, the Navy also had two others off Harwich – Roughs Fort and Sunk Head Fort. But the first of these was not completed until February 1942 – the process of 'springing to arms' being necessarily a lengthy one.

By the time the first of the Maunsell Forts was in operation, there were also twelve 'Eagle Ships' cruising in the estuary. These were flak-ships, but pre-war holiday-makers in Southend would have had little difficulty in recognising them – they were mostly paddle-steamers which had formerly taken them for excursions. Owing to their exceptionally broad beam, they made excellent anti-aircraft gun platforms.

To this mass of fixed and floating artillery were added an extensive balloon barrage, radar-fitted escort vessels, and greatly improved fighter protection; more important, the work of all these was dove-tailed to make the life too difficult and dangerous for the minelayers. But, by the time they did so, the bulk of the Luftwaffe had been for over a year in Russia, leading the advance of the German armies eastward on a thousand mile front, nearly a thousand miles on to Moscow and the Caucasus. The Battle of the Blockade would undoubtedly have been different if Hitler had not made his decision to turn east, the Naval history hints that it might have been fatal; but there can be no certainty of this. The bulk of the German war effort was necessarily devoted to the ground forces and their support; and all of these were useless in face of the Channel. In fact, Hitler had come up against the basic dilemma which confronts the leading land power in Europe. In order to control Europe, the economy must be geared to producing great armies; when these have conquered, they are useless – what is now needed is a great navy. No European power has ever been strong enough to conquer its land neighbours and at the same time maintain a great and superior navy. A part only of the mass of men and material which Hitler sent driving across the eastern plains had any practical application at all to the problems of blockading Britain. They were not a great subtraction from that battle, because the specialised units which alone could strike at our shipping had been left in the west in order to do so. It took two years to defeat them, finally, with of course only a proportion of our war effort – for we were thinking in terms of going back to the continent and of erasing the German cities.

By March 1941, the authorities had woken up to the fact that the blockade was in fact a battle – or, more strictly speaking, a campaign made up of a continuous series of raids – and that it was, for the most part, being fought by civilians on a week-to-week basis. Hardly ever can a major battle have been fought so casually.

Not only had the authorities waging it no control over their forces, but they did not know how many men they had, or what their casualties were, or where reinforcements were to come from; indeed, no arrangements for reinforcements had been made. Every Army Commander, as a matter of course, estimates his casualties in advance and gathers a substantial number of replacements in Reinforcement Holding Units behind the front. Even this can go wrong, if he underestimates battle casualties – as it did in Normandy where, though the assault losses were well below the estimates, they thereafter greatly exceeded them and a reinforcement crisis arose which resulted in the breaking up of divisions.

Consequently, the authorities waging this battle were soon out of their depth from causes not only beyond their control, but beyond their knowledge. They simply did not know what was happening. It was a time to re-fly the famous Mediterranean Fleet signal at the time of the Abyssinian crisis: 'Pro bono publico: no bloody panico.' But in February 1941, a meeting of the National Union of Seamen, presided over by the Minister of Shipping, came to the conclusion that 'The main cause (of the shortage) appeared to be a drift of deck and engine-room ratings to shore occupations'.*

In short, with no casualty or sickness returns to go on, they had jumped to the conclusion that the men were funking it. Indeed, some of the evidence pointed that way. After a particularly rough trip, with perhaps half the convoy destroyed, the masters of the surviving ships might have to look around for a new crew. For any of the officers to duck out, even for one trip, was a matter for contemptuous comment among his former friends; but we have seen how the crews of bombed ships came ashore in a highly nervous state, just as did the survivors from Dunkirk. Most were temporarily 'bomb happy', a few permanently. For the moment, some of them thought they had had enough, and indeed they had. All this is a commonplace of land operations and to meet it, where possible, the three Brigades of a Division are rotated – 'two up and one behind' – and the complete Division is taken out of the line at intervals. Very bad individual cases are evacuated, temporarily, marked down accurately as suffering from 'Battle Exhaustion'. They are in fact, exhausted – nervously – but will recover if rested.†

No such arrangements were made for merchant seamen; instead they made their own, and it was this which caused the uproar and panic. A man may volunteer for one of the Services, but once he had made that decision, he has no further choice; there are Service police and Service prisons and, in the last resort, a Service firing squad if he should waver thereafter. But a merchant seaman was a civilian, without any compulsion except pride and stubborness: he made a new choice every time he sailed; he volunteered weekly, sometimes twice weekly, to go out to the mines and the bombers and the E-boats, to the guns, and the perils of the sea itself.

It was no wonder that men escaped to shore from a sunk or damaged ship took a week or two off from it. There were many sirens on that shore. The man had no protection against his wife, if he had one. Some women don't mind their husbands going off to war; most of them do, particularly if there are children who need a father to look after them. If he was often

* *Merchant Shipping and the Demands of War*, p. 167 (H.M.S.O.).
† For booklength treatment of this subject, by doctors, see Lord Moran's *The Anatomy of Courage* and the *Medical History of the Second World War* (H.M.S.O.).

at home – and, in a coasting job, he would be – he was likely to be faced with a continual urging to give it all up, to think of her and the children. A poor man, with no resources, was particularly vulnerable, as he dreaded leaving his family to the imagined mercy of a faceless clerk in a Government office controlled by a miserly Treasury. And many men would, besides, rather face a complete U-boat pack than continual argument and ill-feeling at home. But many women sent their men away to war, going down to watch the ship sail and wave goodbye – and hid what they felt. They, too, were in the battle and helped to win it.

In the spring of 1941, the authorities clapped down with the Essential Work Order, which gave the Ministry of Labour power to keep merchant seamen at sea, recall others who had taken up shore occupations, and employ at sea men dismissed by the shipowners. And it did not solve their problem. There was still a shortage of men.

They had, in fact, read the situation wrongly; having no facts and figures to go on, they had jumped to obvious – and insulting – conclusions. They had forgotten the dead. In 1940 alone, not including the first three dangerous months of 1941, there were 6,000 merchant seamen dead at sea, besides thousands of others crippled and injured. Probably more than a quarter of the original merchant navy failed to survive the war, or survived it broken in body or mind. The exact figures will never be known, for no returns were made.

Casualties among particular commands of a Service could be higher than this: Bomber Command of the R.A.F., the German U-boat service, and the infantry everywhere, but no Service as a whole would ever be called upon to take losses such as these. But, since they were not a Service, the tendency was to drive them too hard; and, without rest, men all the more quickly reach 'Journey's End'.

The process has never been better depicted than in that play, though the doctors have ably analysed the underlying reasons. The Germans, too, were reaching that point.

Aircraft could be seen nipping in and out of the clouds, over the east coast convoys, obviously nervous and unwilling to press home an attack; they were looking for the smaller ships, which would be lightly armed, or not armed at all. It was a very far cry from the tumultuous stuka attacks pressed to masthead height, of only a year or two ago. Once, a bomber fled from the light on a gun shield. It was sunset, and as the gun swung round, the shield reflected the rays with a brilliant flash of light towards the aircraft, which turned away – thinking it was being fired at! The D.E.M.S. officer who saw this, was very relieved to find that Germans were human after all. But the scene on the decks of the ship were no better.

Guns which required six men to handle them were under-manned, because some of the crew members nominated for the job were below. The two or three men at the gun had to leap around like mad, each one doing several jobs, and in consequence the rate of fire was slow. Sometimes, as the alarm bells kept ringing and the guns fired from the deck above, they would think better of it; and, deciding that they'd better give the lads a hand, came slowly on deck to the gun. One man, who was late in this fashion, got his head above the gun platform just as the gun fired, the muzzle just over his skull. He fell down the ladder, shocked and deafened.

In fact, many of the British and Germans seemed to be afraid of each other; convinced now that it was going to be a long war, that it wasn't their war, and that they were going to survive it. Many of the bravest, naturally, were dead; the survivors went about their job methodically and carefully, but without much interest. The brave days, when war was new and exciting and they were all feeling their oats, were long over; this was no longer the first breathless time, but the hundredth. They intended to live, if they could.

At night, particularly, the strain – the year-long strain – was intense; the night magnifies all peril and one imagines dangers which are not there. On one occasion a convoy passing Flamborough Head was crossed by high-flying bombers, heading west and dropping flares. The convoy went to action stations 'with a clang', as the witness expressed it. Every man, almost, was convinced that this was it, that the bombers were after them. Yet, in fact, nothing at all happened and the planes were probably just dropping flares to check their position on crossing the coast. It is a help if you can put yourself in the position of the poor, miserable enemy – but not all men can do it. In fact, in many men's minds that incident would be recorded as an air attack, as a definite example of peril; just as an army clerk in Normandy sent beetles home to his relatives to prove the horrible conditions which he had to endure. No matter that it was not an attack, it would seem so.

The men who came off best, and lasted longest, were those

who knew exactly when to worry, and shut their minds to danger at all other times; and they were fortunate. And there was danger, all the time; mostly the danger of mines, about which you could do nothing and where only fatalism was of use; and the danger of E-boats, as they neared the Norfolk coast, where a gunner needed to be quick off the mark. Very few men saw an E-boat – the attack came in darkness, was carried out at such speed, and lasted such a short time that it was hard to swear that there had been, in fact, anything there at all. In many cases, there wasn't.

There was a famous Canadian Army cartoon showing a soldier leading in by the leg a small pig from no-man's land, remarking to a Bren gunner in a slit trench that this was the German patrol he had repulsed last night. This is true of all night actions. It is a breathless eerie business to stare out into the night and know that there is an enemy out there, and that he may be coming for you. In the case of the east coast convoys, as they came to the coast of Norfolk in the dark, it expressed itself in a conviction that there were E-boats waiting, tied up to Sheringham buoy, listening for their approach. And an E-boat can slip a torpedo into a merchantman as easily as you can put a knife into the belly of a pig – with much the same effect. Close-range defence was almost always too late. Therefore, when Motor Gun Boat flotillas were formed, they usually operated in defence of the convoys far out to sea; they, too, lay stopped on the routes by which the E-boats must come, in ambush. Many savage little battles took place around Brown Ridge, halfway to Holland, often at dawn, as the E-boat crews crept home exhausted and nervy after their night of strain, and inclined to relax lookout.

But, if there were long, rakish motor craft lying in the swell off Sheringham, waiting for them, there was nothing much the merchantmen could do about it. It was much too late.

The Germans waited inshore of the convoy, alongside the buoys – the witnesses all swear they must have tied up to them – so that they simply started their engines, picked their target, fired torpedoes, and went slap through the convoy at 35 knots or more – headed for home, out of range almost before anyone had a chance to see them. In these waters, the escort fanned out to seaward of the convoy, not to protect it, for that was impossible, but to catch the E-boats as they came through and try to knock one or two for six. It seemed a futile business, to them, but that was not the German impression. Their war diary recorded the comment: 'The British destroyers on the south-east coast know their job.'

On the other hand, they had a poor opinion of the Motor Gun Boats, as indeed the Motor Gun Boats had of them. Neither E-boat nor M.G.B. carried really damaging armament, and in the few seconds for which an engagement lasted, no vital damage could be done; though each side thought they had done it. After a time, they even started ramming each other, in sheer desperation – and that didn't do it. Both sides went happily home, under tow and low in the water, sieved with bullet-holes, to celebrate in the mess the imagined demise of the other. It was fun, but the destroyers were war.

For the merchantmen, just big, bulky, vulnerable targets, it was war indeed. It was very much the same routine in every case. A Naval officer's impression, on one such occasion, was of a lot of indiscriminate firing, with the destroyers putting up starshell and going out to sea as quickly as possible, to catch the speeding E-boats as they came clear of the merchant ships. There was much belching of black smoke, as the firemen piled it on, with the rattling and banging of engines as 8-knot ships started to do 11 knots. He was in one of the merchantmen at the time, and a torpedo was reported to him to be passing ahead. He didn't see it, but it may have been a torpedo, for this was no imaginary attack; a big Dutchman blew up astern, but kept afloat and kept going, at reduced speed. Then it was over – the E-boats had passed through, fired at by the destroyers, and were heading for Holland at top speed, miles away. He never saw one, nor did he see any torpedo tracks. But there was no doubt they had been there.

Another incident was described by a merchant navy gunner. It was 1941, and British M.G.B.s and the motor-launches were helping to escort the convoy. Some of the E-boats were 'hanging on to buoys' inshore of the convoy, but the main attack was from outside. There was a battle going on there, where the British motor-craft were mixing it with the Germans, but it was all too far out to see anything – just tracer and gunflashes flickering over the sea. One E-boat came chasing round the stern, but he couldn't see the thing, only hear it roaring and snarling away as it bumped over the fairly heavy sea then running. Nevertheless, he swung his gun round to where it was going, and then saw in the wash, just a flicker of white moving fast in the darkness. He got away three rounds in a hurry at it, there was a big flash, and then it was all swallowed up in the darkness.

He couldn't claim it, of course, but felt in his bones that he'd got it.

Somewhere, one of the convoy was burning – he seemed to remember that the cargo was whisky; and on the bridge a young Lewis gunner of the 'Maritime' was struggling to load another drum. The bridge was going up and down and pitching, with the motion of the ship in the heavy sea, the soldier was sea-sick and vomiting, almost in tears because the heavy 100-round drum was too much for him in those conditions. He called out to ask where the other gunner was, and the young lad at the Lewis said he thought he was below.

So he was. He was lying down on his bunk, resting. 'Did you hear the alarm, chum?' they asked him. He said yes. 'Did you hear the guns firing?' Yes, he had. But it wasn't his watch, and he wasn't going on deck. The man was a conscript who had dodged his first call-up by going to Eire; he was also very pro-Russian. They reported him to his unit, and – it may have been coincidence only – he was later sent on a Russian convoy. His was an exceptional case, for the 'Maritimes' were very good – they knew their job and they did it.

At the other end of the scale was a 'Maritime' gunner who went to sea three times running – and was sunk on each occasion; the first time by bomb, the second by torpedo, the third by mine. After the third sinking, he was sent home on survivor's leave – and was bombed there, the house being destroyed. He survived that, too; and came up smiling, ready to go to sea again.

In between these two extremes came the mass of sailors in the convoys, most of them civilians still – though the Essential Work Order now gave them regular employment and regular pay, which they had not had before, being 'free' labour. That is, of course, what they were – labourers, electricians, cooks, and so on – not fighting men at all, but committed nevertheless to lose more than a quarter of their number in the face of the enemy.

By 1942, they were hitting back. As one master said, 'We were that well gunned we did not mind what came along.' Most of them kept on sailing, though ship after ship might be damaged or sunk under them, even before authority made it illegal to leave the sea, and at a time when they were little better than targets for the Germans to practice on, as a result of authority's adult delinquency in neglecting the nation's defences. Once properly armed, they got their own back. Captain Hadlow, for instance, whose ship, the *Dona Isabel*, had left him earlier in the war during an E-boat attack, was now master of another collier, the *Grangetoft*.

Their convoy was repeatedly attacked, one day in 1942, by three German aircraft which dived down out of low cloud to bomb, then went up again and circled round for another go. One stick of bombs hurled up the water in foam a hundred feet over on the port bow; then the aircraft came in again to make a job of it, running in at them from the port side low down – about 200 feet above the sea. It was too much for one man who had been bombed and mined and torpedoed for years without a chance to reply. He was the Second Engineer. He pushed the gunner of an Oerlikon out of the way, and grabbed the gun himself, sitting in behind the sights. The Oerlikon was a beautiful gun – you could pop off toy balloons with it, first go.

He let the German plane have the whole drum as it ran up to them and thundered overhead. It started to slant down before it had even crossed the ship and went slap into the sea in a shower of spray a hundred yeards out on the starboard side. They saw it settle in the water, and fall astern of them, with a man climbing out of it, and balancing on the half-submerged fuselage. As the ship next astern passed the wreckage, she fired a long burst and the German crumpled up, his machine vanishing under the water.

It was not cricket, but it was war, illustrative of the pent-up feelings of men kept helplessly under fire for long periods.

Both the other German machines were shot down into the sea, one by a merchantman, the other by a destroyer. Afterwards, the destroyer signalled: 'Good shooting!' But what it was referring to, was anyone's guess.

11 · *Escorts On Top*

ALTHOUGH that area off the Norfolk coast round Sheringham and Yarmouth was known as E-boat Alley – and earned its name – the Germans used the full length of the coastline they had captured to switch attacks from east coast to south coast and back again, whenever it looked as if the escorts were really getting their measure.

In February 1942 the destroyer escort of a southbound convoy came suddenly on a group of eight E-boats up to no good – they were busy laying mines in the path of the convoy. The startled E-boats started off for the horizon in a cloud of smoke, but one, torn to pieces by the destroyers' shells, was sunk, and another was badly damaged. A month later three M.G.B.s of the 7th Flotilla were lying out in the North Sea at night 20 miles off the Dutch coast, when they received reports, thick and fast, from an east coast convoy under E-boat attack. They moved away from the convoy, closer in to the E-boat base at Ijmuiden, and intercepted five of them on the way back. They came back to Lowestoft with M.G.B. 87 flying the Nazi ensign under the white, and eight prisoners on board.

Up to this time the E-boats had been thoroughly enjoying themselves as, apart from the risk of an unlucky brush with a destroyer, there was nothing on our side fast enough, and at the time sufficiently well-armed, to destroy them. But now, an outer screen of M.G.B.s and M.L.s lay to seward of the convoys, through which the E-boats had to come and return. There were not many of them, and production was small, so that a steady loss of one or two boats a month was serious. In June, they moved from their Dutch bases to Cherbourg, in preparation for a surprise attack on a western convoy.

On 7th July, they caught a westbound convoy in Lyme Bay and obtained complete surprise, sinking six of the ships, a total of 12,356 tons. Most of them moved back to Holland, hoping to find the defences off the east coast denuded to protect the south, and there were many savage little night battles, but no smashing success until December. Then, they crept through the outer screen undetected, attacked the northbound convoy F.N. 889, and sank five of them.

But after that, the scales began steadily to tilt against the Germans and it was time to think of reversing 1940 – of attacking them and eventually carrying out our own invasion. To put the German attacks on the east coast convoys in perspective, it should be remembered that the Channel convoys had lost one third of their number, on average, during the worst period of the Battle of the Channel. Losses off the east coast by enemy action from the beginning of the war to mid-November 1942, were 0.247 per cent. 63,350 ships had sailed, and the enemy had managed to sink 157 of them.

A German would not recognise the word 'E-boat', which is hardly surprising, as the term is exclusively English, standing for: 'Enemy War Motorboat'. To him, they are 'S' and 'R' boats, two quite distinct classes. The *Schnellboot* was a fast, torpedo-armed craft capable of 40 knots, equivalent to our M.T.B.s. The *Raumboot* was slower, used for minesweeping, patrol and Air-Sea Rescue, equivalent to our M.L.s. In other words, 'fast-boats' and 'sweeping-boats'. They were low, grey-painted, graceful craft; at dawn, a flotilla of them passing along the horizon was an unforgettably thrilling and beautiful sight. A Coastal Forces officer has described them as looking like 'a flock of widgeon', but he was keen on birds; there was a deadliness about them, too, that would immediately strike an unbiased observer. At slow speed, on a turn, they seemed to hang in the wind on top of the water, only the screws and rudders submerged.

In the beginning, they had to be met by very old destroyers, including some of the 'S' class produced under the Admiralty Emergency War Programme of 1917, as the Emergency War Programme for 1939 had not yet taken effect. The *Sardonyx*, in particular, often escorted Channel convoys through the Straits in 1940. On the east coast many of the 'V. & W.s' (Emergency War Programme 1916-18) kept to the seas in all weathers; old, but once the best destroyers of their time, they herded the merchantmen up and down the swept channels, collecting and delivering them at the various ports. The crews worked exhausting watches, four hours on and four hours off, with 'action stations' constantly sounded. In winter, the mountainous seas buried the bows deep under and swept the men on the bridge with the shock of bitterly cold water; down below, in the mess decks, there was chaos, with kit and gear slopping about in a mass of sea-water, and somebody's shaving brush falling from a rack, like a well-thrown dart, into the jam-pot; and the tea thrown into the men's laps. There was nothing that was not moving, nothing that stayed still; the world heaved and rolled all the time; on the bridge the look-outs would be soaked to the skin and the men below would be continually banged against the sides of the ship and any sharp projection that was handy.

When they had seen the convoy safely in, they would enter the harbour, usually at mid-day; there would be a few hour's leave for the off-duty watch, ashore, on something that wasn't pitching and rolling, while the duty watch refuelled and provisioned the destroyer. Then out to sea again at midnight, to shepherd another convoy through the darkness; perhaps passing a convoy steaming in the opposite direction, with big ships suddenly coming out of the blowing darkness of the gale, and looming high above them. That was the most of it, but to some of them came the roar of mine or torpedo – and 'abandon ship' in a raging sea off a bleak coast. The *Vimiera* and the *Whitshed* were both mined off the east coast early in 1942, and sunk. In March, the *Vortigern* was sunk by a torpedo from an E-boat. They bore the brunt of it until the new destroyers were ready.

The original supply of volunteer gunners for D.E.M.S. had long ago been used up; most of them now had commissions. To ensure that high standards of efficiency were kept up, inspecting officers from the D.E.M.S. staff took periodical trips in merchant ships. One of these officers, Lt-Comdr H. Ruddy, R.N.V.R., took passage in a Channel convoy leaving Southend for the Straits. As the coaster steamed out into the estuary ready for forming up, and the battered wrecks went past on either hand, he left the bridge to inspect the gunners; to see what sort of a watch they kept, how they kept their guns, and how good they were with them.

The guns were there all right, and probably they would have fired, in spite of the dirt; but there were no gunners near them. So he went in haste to their quarters – but they weren't there either. He climbed the bridge ladder in a fury, to ask the master where they had got to. The master looked quite blank, then pointed to a sailor standing in the wing of the bridge – a not-too-clean young man in a football jersey with red stripes. 'There's one of 'em,' he said.

On another occasion, testing the capacities of a man with a gunner's badge up, he discovered that he did not know how to strip the gun. He told him to stay on the gun platform until he had found out. It took the 'gunner' two hours, but he did it in the end. The trouble was that some of the conscripts, unlike the volunteers before them, simply couldn't be bothered to carry on learning the job on their own. Tom, Dick and Harry were drafted in a hurry to do the job, and though Tom and Dick might be all right, Harry preferred to take it easy, even at the risk of his life.

But the worst job he ever had to do was with the best gun's crew he ever saw. The Acting Petty Officer in charge was smart as a whistle in peaked cap and brass buttons, the gun's crew were quick and alert, the gun was spotless, and they knew how to handle it. The Petty Officer's pride in himself and his uniform had obviously helped him in his job and braced the morale of his men; clearly, they could be in action within split-seconds in waters where split-seconds mattered. But the P.O. was not entitled to his uniform. He had the rank, but as a 'Hostilities Only' man, he was not allowed to wear the cap and brass buttons and had obviously bought them himself out of his pay. If the uniform went, some of that split-second polish might go, too; but it had to be done. It was the hardest decision he had ever had to take.

D.E.M.S. grew rapidly from about 2,000 men to 35,000 in a short time and, besides inspecting officers in the ships, a lot of weight was put in at the top to ensure efficiency. The Inspector of Merchant Navy Gunnery was now a Vice-Admiral, or even a full Admiral, with under him a gunnery Commander; also another Commander whose job was to interview the masters, if they had survived, of every ship sunk or damaged, in order to keep continually in touch with German methods and the effectiveness of the counter-measures.

One inspecting officer was most unfortunate in his choice of ship. It was a collier, sailing from the Thames with an experienced pilot, a lean, quiet man who looked as if he knew his job, which indeed he did. However, another ship came suddenly straight across their bows, so that they could do nothing else but hit it. Repairs took one week, and the master was very cast down; although it was not his fault, it was his first time in command and he felt it very keenly.

When they sailed again, the convoy met thick fog in E-boat Alley and they lost sight of the other ships. The vessel shivered slightly, then glided on; there were several more harsh bumps under the keel, and it came to a dead stop, the screws threshing the water unavailingly. They were firmly on the dreaded Haisborough Sands which, as everyone knew perfectly well, had claimed seven ships in one night, with the loss of thirty-seven men.

On this occasion, too, there was a heavy sea running, and the crew expected her to break up at once. It was a dreadful moment for a master, on the first voyage in his first command; and at that moment some of the crew, without waiting for any orders from him, started to lower away a boat.

A short, choppy sea was pounding the ship and her plates were groaning under the strain; foam was hissing over the sands, and all around them stretched a vicious chaos of tossing, spray-torn water. The boat lasted less than two minutes, rearing and plunging violently, then it turned over. By desperate exertions, they saved the men in it, but the boat, waterlogged, was driven away to be pounded to pieces on the sands. That, too, would be their fate, they felt, but there was nothing now to do but wait for the end.

However, the fog lifted shortly after, and they could see that, far from being hopelessly stranded on the sands, they were only a few hundred yards from the channel. With a little careful manoeuvring and a lot of full-speed astern, they slipped off quite easily. But the master was in a fit of despair; holding his head between his hands, he lamented the damage – at the very least the double bottom must have been ripped and the hull in a terrible mess, with started plates everywhere. It would be his last command.

When the collier was dry-docked, inspection revealed that not one single rivet had been started, and there were no complaints about that. There was, however, an unholy row about the lost lifeboat!

Many colliers, of course, such as this one, never normally went to the south coast at all; they plied steadily between the coal ports and London. Battersea Power Station alone consumed enormous quantities of solid fuel and a fleet of colliers was required to supply it. There were many foreigners among them, sometimes as high as 20 per cent of the ships were not British; and this added spice to the verbal exchanges, by loud-hailer or plain shouting, with which the escorts and the merchantmen enlivened the danger and tedium of the passage, especially as Tyneside-manned colliers were virtually incomprehensible even to an Englishman. As the ships steamed along the east coast at an average speed of four knots, stragglers catching up in the darkness would hail the next ahead: 'Any Geordies aboard that ship?' And get, perhaps, the reply: 'Naw – only North Sea Chinamen!'

If the other vessel was a foreigner, mutual bafflement could follow, as in the case where a Geordie hailed a Norwegian collier, the *Anna*.

From the Tynesider came: 'What ship?' and from the Norwegian: 'An-nah!' Puzzled, the Geordie repeated: 'What ship?' and the Norwegian promptly replied 'An-nah!' At which the Geordie bellowed out, exasperated: 'Ar knaw, yer knaw, but we divn't!'

The tones of the escort, rounding up stragglers or pointing out faults, were quite different; professional destroyers were well-educated and preferred best to score off each other with an appropriate Latin tag or judiciously selected reference to a particular paragraph in the Bible. This was no help at all as far as the colliers were concerned, who dearly loved to put the proper Navy out of its stride. On a night when thunder boomed over the seas and lightning intermittently lit up the ships, most of the balloons caught fire and were lost; nevertheless, in the morning, an escort vessel came rolling alongside the convoy, from ship to ship, asking what had happened to its balloon. The second ship to be asked, a Tyneside collier, caught on quickly and answered at once: 'Ar swopped it for a couple of jam jars last night.'

This same collier, going on to the Channel in a convoy which was caught by fog at night, was forced to anchor not far from the German-held coast. It was 1942, and the Germans were still sending over minelayers to our swept channels. At first, there was nothing to be heard out in the fog except the normal dismal sounds of the sea at such a time, and every noise they made seemed magnified. Then they heard a ship approaching slowly from the direction of the French coast. It, too, seemed baffled by the fog and hung about near them. Nothing could be seen but the swirling banks of vapour, but they could hear voices from the other vessel. They were certainly not English, the language seemed very like German; but the chilling point was that the stranger was obviously a warship. The various orders came crisply, and to a set pattern; the replied flicked back smartly.

The collier master ordered every man to take off his shoes and walk about in his socks, so that the stranger, whoever he might be, should have no clue to their presence. Promptly a fireman dropped a shovel – in the tense stillness aboard the fog-bound collier, it sounded like a clap of thunder. There was a surprised howl of: 'Quiet!'

But, in spite of all their efforts, the strange vessel had heard them. For, when the fog cleared at dawn – to reveal a Norwegian warship almost alongside – her commander popped up on her bridge and observed, politely: 'I think we have been lying alongside you all night, Captain!' The collier master's reply was brief: 'I think you —— —— have!'

The colliers were often led out by a row of trawler minesweepers but, by 1943, when the tide had turned, some of these were employed for deception purposes and as convoy escorts. Their job was at the other end of the scale to that of the M.G.B.s of Coastal Forces, whose task was not too exacting, fun, and well publicised. Coastal Forces were the prima donnas, and the minesweepers the patient ploughmen, of the Channel. The irksome point was that a really high standard of skill was required of the minesweepers whereas anyone, within reason, could handle and navigate a big, fast motor-boat. If the navigator botched it, and was half a mile out, it hardly mattered; but if a minesweeper was only yards out it could mean the end, for the minesweeper, or for someone else. Furthermore, the work of Coastal Forces was aggressive and exiting as well as dangerous; the work of the minesweepers was deadly dull, and deadly dangerous.

Two types of men commanded the minesweepers. The R.N.V.R. officers, drawn mainly from the people who messed around in boats for pleasure, were highly intelligent, with plenty of education and theory. They were extremely conscientious and worried away at their problems. The R.N.R. officers, drawn from people who had always made their living by the sea, never worried, they just went at their problems head down, like a bull at a gate. They had no idea at all of scientific navigation; they just guessed; and they guessed right. It wasn't luck, it was a sixth sense. Their motto was: 'Down anchor – down head'. In a tumult of tossing water, off a lee shore, they could find a little haven in between the banks, and lie there all night, snug as a bug in a rug. One very nearly came unstuck, when the anchor parted from the cable and the trawler drifted steadily towards the rocks with everyone aboard sleeping soundly. With fifteen minutes to go, before they were due to be lost, they all came yawning on deck, and hauled in the anchor cable – to find a frayed end and no anchor! They had got away with it again, as they usually did.

The collier master and his officers were of this breed; but, being in convoy, no longer had the opportunity to use to the full the skill and knowledge bred in them, they merely had to follow like sheep.

Sometimes a sweep had barely started, before they began

to put up mines, far and near. Once the armed trawler *Hornbeam* put one up before it had started at all. Her captain, Lt-Comdr Matthews, D.S.C., M.M., R.N.V.R., had been a soldier in the first world war. As the leader started to flash: 'Open out and sweep,' he had his head over the chart table. Standing beside him was a Liverpool lawyer, accompanying him for skipper experience before taking over his own trawler. And at that moment the trawler went right over to starboard, from the impact of a mine that had gone up 100 feet away on the port side. Matthews and the lawyer, who was well-built, cannoned violently together. The *Hornbeam* slowly righted and as she did so a mass of water from the mine explosion thumped down on the forecastle, and poured off down the small hatch that led to the crews' sleeping quarters. Most of them were down there, eating, shaving or sleeping. The water came down on them solidly, and most of them thought they were on the bottom already, there was so much sea bursting in.

They came up that hatch like corks out of a bottle. One had a shaving brush in his hand, his face was lathered; another was holding a slice of bread and jam; and a third was in his pyjamas; and they were all scared stiff, believing themselves in need of submarine escape apparatus.

The trawlers' work was methodical, accurate, and usually done in company. They went to the channel to be swept in line ahead and then opened out into sweeping formation, sweeping first for magnetics, then for acoustics – and taking care to switch on the sweep before they came to the suspected area, to avoid sending one up underneath themselves. There was no telling where an acoustic mine might go up, it depended on the setting. If the mine was set for a small ship, then the powerful impulse of the sweep might put it up two miles away; but, if set to catch a big ship, the trawler might be on top of it before the thing reacted. This uncertainty turned a sweeper into a pariah, whose company was shunned by all.

For instance, an M/S trawler was flashed by a destroyer: 'Are you acoustic?' When the sweeper replied that she was, the destroyer flashed back: 'Keep away from me!'

There were, however, advantages in being a sweeper. On one occasion the *Hornbeam* flashed to a destroyer: 'You are in our course.' There was no reply, and the destroyer kept on as before. Regular R.N. officers, said Matthews, were usually 'gentlemen and diplomats', but some of the jumped-up ones were 'pigs'. This one was a pig. He ignored repeated signals, then the sweep unexpectedly put up a mine a few hundred yards from him, and 'you couldn't see his stern for dust'.

The fishing trawlers encountered off the east coast and else-where were often literally asleep. Once one of them ignored the sweep balls flown by the minesweeper to indicate that she was at work; ignored signals, flashes and hails – and when the sweeper closed with her, she found the decks deserted; the crew were all below, with their heads down! The reason was that all the best men had been taken out of the fishing fleets for the Navy, those left were very careless. One of them happily picked up a mine and beetled over to the nearest destroyer, to shout at it through a megaphone: 'Hey, mister, I've got a mine on deck – what shall I do with it?' To which the destroyer loud-hailed back: 'Give me five minutes start – and you can do what you like with it!'

The gadget used for sending up acoustic mines consisted of a ponderous 'A' frame and hammer fitted to the sweeper's bows. One of the new motor minesweepers was coming into a lock, at Liverpool when, so the skipper said, he ordered half astern and got half ahead. The 'A' frame and hammer went slap through the lock gate, and the sweeper bounced back from the impact. An old boy stuck his head out of a hut ashore and observed: 'If you'd told me you wanted to come in, sir, I'd have opened the door for you. Heee-e!'

All sweepers got very fat on fish, and the crews were very keen on it, due to the wartime scarcity. The putting up of a mine was usually followed by the time-hallowed ritual of: 'Put a boat over, sir?' followed by an instantaneous affirmative. The *Hornbeam*'s captain, acting on a sudden instinctive premonition, once refused, with a sharp: 'No, nothing doing.' The crew were very incensed, as the trawler circled the vortex of troubled water where the mine had gone up, thinking of all the fish it must have killed. Then the water rose up in a great spurt to the sky – another mine!

Then, some distance away, they saw something huge and white, flapping in the water. It was safe now to put the boat over, and what it towed back was a giant cod, stunned by the second explosion. They had to hook him through the gills to get him on board – he had seven flatfish inside him and he weighed 34 lbs.

The *Hornbeam*'s captain was once introduced to the King and Queen. All ships in dock had been painted – on one side only; the men to be introduced had been briefed – 'Your Majesty' the first time, 'Sir' thereafter; and Lt-Comdr Matthews stepped forward very smartly to be introduced, and stepped backwards equally smartly afterwards, but unfortunately too far, almost into the dock. The King shot out his hand, grabbed him by the shoulder, and hauled him back with a: 'Look out, man, you'll be over!' Then he asked him what his job was and when Matthews replied 'Mine-sweeping', the Queen interjected: 'A dangerous job.'

The King turned to her and explained: 'Dangerous and *monotonous*; they have to sweep every channel at least fifteen times.'

That one sentence put up the morale of the minesweepers a hundred per cent. It *was* monotonous, that was the deadly, depressing part of it; but to realise that the King actually knew accurately the details of their job bucked them up wonderfully, particularly as the local C-in-C (Max Horton) had been reported as saying, contemptuously, 'Oh, have we got minesweepers, too!' when the list of ships was put before him.

By 1943 the situation was well under control and it was possible to release some of the sweepers for other work. A great deception plan was under way, to fool the Germans about the coming invasion, the real preparations for which were going on everywhere along the south coast. These trawlers, the *Hornbeam* among them, put in to Tilbury to collect barges which they towed through the Channel, trailing them under the noses of the Germans in the Straits and delivering them to Portsmouth, Poole, Portland and other likely invasion harbours. When the trawlers returned, they did so as escort vessels to the colliers and other coasters in the various convoys bound to the east.

Larger ships were now using the Channel, Plymouth was once more in use as a major naval base, and big events were under way. The Germans knew very well what was impending, and did their level best to harry the convoys.

But the main worry of the trawler captains was lack of sleep. Normally, they only carried two officers, the junior staying in the ship until he became efficient – and then being sent away to take over his own command – so that the captain had to start again from scratch with a brand-new 'Number One' just out of *King Alfred*. It was the same, even with the cooks: as soon as they were up-rated, they were off. So the captain carried a tremendous responsibility.

There was no-one to turn to, if he himself was unsure. He had to give the appearance of confidence, of knowing exactly what to do, even if he had no idea what was going to happen next, or what to do about it. He couldn't confide in anyone, and he couldn't relax. And he was the ship's doctor as well.

The armed trawlers came out of Tilbury very early in the morning, at about 6 o'clock, after the captains had already attended a conference on shore. A tug brought out to them their two barges. These looked very like the real thing – but they weren't. They were ordinary barges, with the bows cut out to take ramps, exactly the sort of vessels the Germans had assembled for their intended invasion – and virtually useless for that purpose. The real, specialised craft for the landings were quite different.

The captain was on the bridge all the way down to the Goodwins, as it was impossible to hand over in those difficult waters to an inexperienced First Lieutenant. At the Goodwins, he was still on the bridge, for this was where the westward and the eastward convoys crossed. He was still on the bridge at Dover, because of the danger of E-boats and fighter-bombers. Fighter cover was good now, but the Germans used often to watch when the patrolling planes turned for home, and take their place – coming at the convoy from the landward side, perhaps unidentified until the last moment.

The balloons would be pulled down, to avoid giving the guns a ranging target. The racket of the shelling was unnerving – but nothing worse. The sound of our own guns firing overhead was more unnerving than that of the enemy's, particularly as the captain would be jumpy from lack of sleep. After Dover, he turned in – for a few hours.

His sleep might be interrupted in any number of ways. Radar watched the Germans closely, and if E-boats or suspicious aircraft came over, they would warn them of possible mines – and that meant alterations of course. If he was not interrupted, he would come on deck again when they were approaching Selsey Bill. They came in close to the land, with many treacherous sandbanks in the vicinity; also, the fighter-bombers liked this area. When off Hayling, radar might warn: 'Air attack coming in now'. And right on the heels of the warning an Me 109 or F.W. 190 would come from the north, screaming over the holiday camps and the barbed wire and concrete blocks on the beaches, to blast with cannon and machine-gun fire at the trawlers and the barges it was trailing as a coat.

The lookouts would have to be watched; since they looked, but did not see. They were inexperienced, mostly conscripts, and could easily miss a buoy or an aircraft, even when gazing at it. In this way, they carried on down to Portland and delivered the barges. At Portland, they would pick up an east-bound convoy and sail back with it, as additional escort.

Once, they came into a belt of very thick fog; they could see nothing, but kept the same course and speed, hoping that everyone else would be doing the same and that there would be no collisions. Somewhere off West Bay, firing began. They could hear the rattle of machine-guns and cannon, and now the escort were helpless. The fighter-bombers were circling above the fog-bank and diving to fire at the masts which they could see sticking up through it; but no-one could see them and there was no target and no chance of an accurate reply. One of the trawlers was badly shot up, punctured everywhere. A cannon shell went through the minesweeping gear, another wounded a seaman, and a third ripped into the Captain's cabin. He was dressing when the attack began, and hadn't hoisted up his trousers; but the cannon shell took no notice – it slapped through the side of the trawler, skimmed where his trousers ought to have been, and went out of the trawler by the other side.

This convoy was a mixed bag – not all colliers, and not all British, either. Many of them either couldn't or wouldn't understand signals. When they came to where the Needles ought to have been, there were no Needles – just fog. This was where some of the convoy should have dispersed into the Solent, the remainder – and possibly 'joiners' from the Motherbank – carrying on up Channel. Near them, a Dutch ship came in sight; she positively refused to stop and carried on alone, obviously fed up with the dangers and delays of the convoy. A large number of ships were loose in the fog, unable to anchor in the swept channel for fear of being kicked up the stern by someone else's bow, afraid to move out to sea because of the protective belt of our own minefield, and with their masts sticking up above the fog bank as an open invitation to the fighter-bombers to 'come and get me some time'. The Dutchman was well out of it, scuttling on to Shoreham as fast as he dare go.

If any man was wounded, it might be a long time before he saw a doctor; in the meantime the Captain was expected to see to him. Once, they saw a ship go up on a mine and were first on the spot. There were three bodies floating in the water. There was the Captain of the ship, but he was dead, and two members of the crew who had been down below when the explosion occurred. Curiously, no one who had been on deck had survived, but these two had. One of them, a stoker, had a big gash in his wrist, which needed attention. They managed to transfer him to a larger ship, which had a doctor. Most ships did not carry them, but a Surgeon Probationer or even a steward was better than the Captain's semi-practised skill, for he loathed the job. But, in a trawler, he was the only one who knew anything at all about it; though that didn't seem to worry the crews.

A man would roll up with a fish-hook in his hand, to be anaesthetised in the Nelson fashion. The only modern touch was that the fluid was not rum but whisky; after he'd had a couple of straight glasses he wouldn't feel much. The skipper whispered for a bowl of hot water and (very low) a pair of pliers. When they were brought, he turned to the man with the fish-hook and advised him to put his hand in the hot water to remove the dirt; as he did so, breathing whisky from both nostrils, the skipper grabbed him by the arm, got a grip of the protruding part of the fish-hook with the pliers – and pulled! Out came the fish-hook, as well as a lot of blood and flesh, but the job was done – and the man had felt little or nothing.

For the Germans the writing was already on the wall. As early as May 1942, the convoys had had evidence of it. On the night of the 30th/31st, an eastbound convoy was passing through the Straits of Dover, with above them a small stream of German bombers flying inland and another stream of bombers pouring endlessly out from England towards the continent, bound for Cologne as part of the first thousand-bomber raid. Strictly speaking, though the German effort that night was a raid, the R.A.F. operation was an assault. And when one ship of the convoy opened up at the German bombers passing overhead, some of them abandoned their more dangerous target inland and came down on the ships. The convoy was shaken up, but no real damage was done.

In the first half of 1943, the E-boats sank two ships (6,580 tons) and lost two of their number, one to the destroyers, the other to the M.G.B.s. It was not a favourable rate of exchange. The Commander-in-Chief, Portsmouth, had said of some merchant skippers he had met in 1942:

'Their courage and determination is beyond all praise. Week after week, year after year, they go plugging up and down the Channel, never knowing when a dive-bomber or an E-boat is going to appear and send them to the bottom. Great men!'(*)

That ordeal was now drawing to its close; the period when, ill-armed or unarmed, we defended ourselves. Now we were

* Admiral Sir William James, *The Portsmouth Letters.*

going over to the attack, and with the assault forces were to go the colliers.

The great deception utterly failed: it was a bait which the Germans did not take – they watched the barges go by in stony silence. Other activity they did not notice, or misinterpreted, not knowing what to look for and with their eyes anyway turned always to the Pas de Calais. That, they were convinced, was where the invaders would land – the shortest sea route, well within fighter range, the route they themselves had chosen. Hitler himself fancied Norway. But the real centre of gravity of the invasion lay in the area of the Portsmouth Command. In the backwaters of the Beaulieu river and in the mudflats of Langstone Harbour and on the shores of Hayling Island a horde of dredgers were at work. They were digging pits in the mud and sand – and tugs fussed in, towing big, floating oblong blocks, huge steel boxes, which they manoeuvred into the berths dug in the mud. And there, they were sunk. Off Selsey Bill, feverish activity was taking place under the gaze of a few holiday-makers who lay in the sun on those once-crowded beaches. What was taking place looked to them like a mirage. A line of masts, or what seemed to be masts, stretched out into the Channel from Selsey Bill, pointing towards the French coast. Even at that distance, they seemed enormous, and there were more of them behind the hills of the Isle of Wight. They were moving slowly all the time, with balloons flying above them, and all along the water was a mass of giant objects, also moving slowly. They stretched out from Selsey Bill like the arm of some gigantic meccano harbour conceived on a fantastic scale; and that is exactly what they were. Next day they were gone. They lay on the bottom, on the sand banks off Selsey, awaiting their hour, their day. And that day would be D-Day.

12 · *Wheezing And Dodging*

A VIVID flash shot out from the stern of the French collier, rolling in convoy, and a dirty great cloud of oily smoke went spouting up the sky. The ships were under air attack, and it seemed to her consorts that the collier must have been mortally hit by a bomb. Yet she steamed on, seemingly unperturbed, her speed unreduced. No one else knew at the time, that the tremendous roll of smoke was from a new and secret anti-aircraft weapon with which she had been fitted.

It is a problem to imagine who was the most terrified – the German airmen at whom it was fired, or the crew of the ship which fired it; but the probability is that it was the latter. An extremely spectacular weapon, it had been developed by the Army under conditions of the greatest secrecy. The Admiralty became interested and an officer from D.E.M.S. received orders to take a train from Waterloo to the testing area. Virtually blind-folded and handcuffed, he was at length brought to the secret weapons testing site.

Here, he was shown into a room where he was issued with gum-boots and then led out into what had once been a field but was now an indescribably smelly mess of mud and oil, mixed. The 'Thing' stood in front of him. It looked like an exact, true-scale replica of the funnel of Stevenson's Rocket. That is, it was a long black tube with a fringe at the top. Out of it, when fired, came flame and smoke – the latter in great quantities. The weight, he learned with interest, was one ton.

After seeing the secret weapon in action, he went back and wrote a lengthy report to the Admiralty, which may be summarised briefly as: 'No, No, a Thousand Times, No!'

But the Admiralty, forward-looking, and perhaps not wanting to be held up to further ridicule in the popular press as un-progressive retrogrades, decided that the weapon should at least be given the courtesy of a trial; and two of them were, in fact, fitted to merchant ships. The masters of both ships noticed, with interest, that the weight was one ton. They also used a lot of bad language, but that has no place here.

101

One of the two ships so fitted – alas, no one now can recall her name – made only one trip with the 'Thing' on board. When the ship discharged her cargo, she also discharged the 'Thing'. It was discovered, much later, sitting quietly in an obscure part of the docks – as secret as it could possibly be. The Admiralty took the hint – much to the relief of the merchantmen.

The fact is that the British people had risen to their great crisis in 1940, not only as people, but as individuals. Burning to strike a blow in this, their finest hour, they had taken any means that came to hand. Actual participation in the battle was impossible. You couldn't very well build yourself a Spitfire in the back garden, fill it up with low-grade petrol syphoned from your neighbour's car, and thunder off to join the fight. But the will to do so was there.

It was a period of killing Hitler with your mouth, since there was really very little else to slaughter him with. Some few dedicated individuals, however, and some of them even before the war, went further: with feverish ingenuity they dreamt up novel weapons which should take the place of the conventional articles of which we had not nearly enough. Far away then were the days when we had more Bofors guns than the Germans had aircraft. In any case, conventional weapons were under something of a cloud at that time. It was widely believed, quite erroneously, that the German successes could be due only to strange, new, and utterly outlandish weapons which had confounded their enemies by the stunning shock of surprise and terror. Actually, the Germans had used only conventional weapons – quite a proportion of their Divisional transport was moved by that product of high-powered modern science, the horse.

The tank – we invented that; paratroops – the Russians invented those; the dive-bomber – copies from the Yankee 'Helldiver' – there had even been a Hollywood epic about it; the E-boat – Lawrence of Arabia and the Power Boat Company had been first there (the Germans were trying to sell us E-boats in 1939 – we weren't interested). Nothing was new but the use – and even that had been predicted and urged upon both the British and the French by some of their own generals. Nevertheless, the barrage of accusations hurled, quite rightly, against old-fashioned methods did create a climate in which new-fangled weapons were regarded with rather more interest than they would otherwise have been.

Some of these bore fruit; some didn't. And there were many

borderline cases with which the front-line merchantmen, long-suffering as ever, were inflicted. At best, perhaps they were better than bare hands; perhaps some German pilots were slightly off-put, or did not press on down to low level because they knew that the perfidious, egg-headed English had entanglements ready for them.

There was really quite a bright idea known as the Holman Projector, virtually a compressed-air mortar, cheap and quick to build, using a projectile already in quantity production – the '36' grenade. The grenade – oval and rather larger than a cricket ball – was highly conventional, having been used as an infantry weapon in two world wars. As millions of men know, you just pull out the pin, count three or four according to the strength of your nerves, chuck it, and four seconds or so later comes the bang.

With the Holman Projector, the gunner picked up a '36' grenade, pulled out the pin, popped the grenade down the barrel of the Projector, pressed a switch with his foot, and a blast of compressed air and steam hurled the grenade up into the path of an attacking bomber where – after an indefinite number of seconds – it burst.

The grenade didn't go very far, and if the Chief Engineer was mean about the steam, it went even less. It might even, if he had been particularly mingy, roll lazily up the barrel and collapse with a sigh upon the deck – due to explode in about five seconds from now. Holman Projector gunners got very adept at the footballer's side-sweep. With plenty of practice – and they got it – the grenade could be kicked over the side with at least two seconds to spare before it exploded.

Additionally, in the heat of action, with stukas hurtling at the ship and bomb splinters screaming round the gun position, it was easy to miss the barrel altogether. For real effectiveness, the Projector relied on a perfect stream of grenades sailing up into space and bursting just underneath the Jerry pilot's pants. To get this rate of fire, the drill was: out pin, drop, press – swoosh! – out pin, drop, press – swoosh! – and so on, in rapid sequence. Many a time the loader – gazing up at the swooping plane and with machine-gun bullets crackling round his ears – in fact, working at speed and under stress, missed his stroke completely and dropped the armed grenade on the deck. For a few seconds, there would be chaos, with a crowd of amateur footballers trying to heel the thing over the side before it burst.

Because we are a Soccer-playing nation, casualties from this cause were almost unknown – and so were German. What was wanted, to really make the inventor's dream work, was lots of practice: and many gun crews did in fact manfully put in many hours, firing potatoes out of the Projector – until the cook discovered what was happening.

There was also the P.A.C., invented shortly before the war. The initials do not mean what they mean in the Army – they stood for Parachute and Cable Projector. Two were usually fitted, one in either wing of a merchantman's bridge. They were fired by a lanyard – if the gunners kept the cartridges dry; if they didn't, they wouldn't. But if they did, a long length of wire cable went snaking prettily up into the sky. At the top of its trajectory, a little parachute burst merrily into view on cue, and lowered the cable ever so gently onto the sea. German pilots were supposed to run into it, and wrap the cable round their props. There is a recorded instance of this actually happening – at an aerodrome during the Battle of Britain.

Stories about the P.A.C. always end with the one about the man – drunk or sober – who fired the thing and wrapped himself in several hundred yards of cable and a parachute. The only variant is by a minesweeper which wrapped it round her screw and nearly sunk herself. Such stories, of such unanimous complexion, are extraordinarily significant, the equivalent of the soldier's judgement on the Sten – that it only fired when you put it down.

The official histories skate delicately over the subject, piercing to the heart with faint praise. The fact is that no-one really liked the wheezes and dodges; not even thoughtful effort to give bridge protection were appreciated. At first sight, the development of plastic armour for the ship's officers, sailors and gunners exposed on the bridge seemed to offer a great improvement. Unfortunately, in hot weather, some types of plastic armour literally melted away; others, if disturbed by a bomb, swept the bridge with lethal fragments.

The weapon really needed, which the colliers got in the end, was the Oerlikon – an 0.79-inch quick-firing cannon; virtually a large machine-gun, firing a small shell. There was nothing fussy about it, no trace of wild genius; it merely did the job. Put a bad gunner behind an Oerlikon, and he became at that instant a good gunner; put a German in front of it, and he was likely to become a dead German in short order. It was thoroughly conventional, but because it was a precision weapon it could not be produced in a hurry, unlike 'gas-pipe guns'.

But, before they could get the magnificent Oerlikon, ship's gunners had to make do, not only with the weird and wonderful, but with a long procession of basically unsuitable light machine-guns. There was nothing much against the Hotchkiss, except that if the barrel-locking nut wasn't very carefully watched, the barrel fell off; nor against the Lewis, except that if not carefully maintained and the drums very carefully loaded, it jammed; there may have been nothing wrong with the American Marlin – intended for a different purpose, hurriedly whipped out of aircraft and sent across the Atlantic under Lend/Lease – but the British gunners never did get the hang of it; and there was certainly nothing wrong with the Bren – except that this also was an L.M.G., with neither punch nor range. The most one could reasonably expect was a deterrent effect. The enemy, being a human being, was likely to flinch if fired at; he would be less likely to press home his attack, less likely to hit.

The Lewis-gunner who did shoot down an enemy had every right to be pleased with himself – it was incredible, and should not have happened. The successes we have recorded tend to be as misleading as reading a succession of fighter pilots' combat reports on the monotonous theme of: 'Wacko – and another Nazi bit the dust.' One feels sorry for the poor, miserable enemy; one forgets that these are the reports of men who came back – not of those who didn't; for the dead are dead, and tell no tales. If they could, it would not be of victory.

Most gunners never killed. They fired thousands of rounds and lessened in some degree the danger of enemy attack; they did what they were expected to do, and many – whose tales will never be told – were still doing it when the ship rolled over and went down. And these, too, were not without honour.

13 · Oddentification

THE Beaufighter was low down over the water, racing for home. A few feet above the canopy, and perhaps fifty feet above the water, was the cloud base. Clammy fingers of mist, lower than the rest, appeared ahead, shot past, and were gone. The water below was cold, grey, sullen. It lay in a circle around the aircraft – at least, that is what the pilot saw. His view, restricted in any case by nose, engines, and wings, was limited below by the mist to a circle of grey sea perhaps 150 yards in diameter. And that circle of visibility was moving with him towards the English coast at 250 m.p.h.

Straight ahead, the side of a ship appeared, leaping from a dark shadow to a high rust-streaked hull, shedding tendrils of fog, in a second or two and seeming, to the pilot, to come at him at 250 m.p.h. A thoughtful man would have considered, soberly, what to do – and would have been dead. The pilot did not think, he pulled the stick right back in one convulsive movement and, fascinated, saw the ship's wireless aerial go down just below his flashing airscrews; then he eased forward gently to where the circle of visible sea was coming into view again; and went through the inner line of ships with hardly a shot fired at him, and those more in warning than in anger.

He had survived an encounter with a Channel convoy. They were a menace to all pilots, British and German, incautious enough to come near them, especially so in the latter half of the war when their armament had become formidable. They fired at anything which approached them in what appeared to them to be a 'hostile manner'; in practice that meant any aircraft anywhere near. The ships took the view that if they fired at the aircraft, they probably wouldn't hit it first time anyway: that, if British, it would take the hint and sheer off; if German it might be discouraged or at any rate disturbed on its bombing run. And it would not be too unkind to assume that most sailors were vague about the difference between the Wright Biplane and the Graf Zeppelin and that airmen, for their part, might easily confuse a powerful tug with the *Queen Mary*.

Much unnecessary heat was generated by this, for aircraft

and ship recognition were separate and tricky subjects, requiring almost a lifetime of devoted study. People who grew up with ships could tell a *V. & W.*-class destroyer while it was still on the horizon, people who grew up with aeroplanes could identify a new German type, first shot, many miles away. And neither could understand the apparent imbecility of the other when operating outside his own special sphere of knowledge.

This situation continued throughout the war, regardless of the considerable efforts made by all three Services to teach the man-on-the-job the elements of his trade. They made not the slightest impression. Ignorance continued, to the end, invincible and unteachable. The R.A.F. dared not give fighter cover to convoys at night, because of the certainty that their aircraft would be fired at, though it was the practice of some D.E.M.S. officers to greet applicants for leave from behind a desk littered with aircraft models and the formula: 'So you want leave?'

'Yessir.'

The officer would pick up at random one of the models from his desk. 'Tell me what this is.'

The gunner would stare, horrified and transfixed, at the little black wooden replica of an aircraft. 'I dunno, sir.'

'When you *can* tell me what it is – you can put in another application for leave. And not before.'

Even if the models and books of silhouettes could be memorised, there was still no real certainty. Aeroplanes didn't look like that, except when very high, or very far away; and the monoplanes of the second world war were very alike. Much the most distinctive point, incapable of being conveyed by book-learning, was the 'sit' – the angle at which the aircraft, so to speak, took the air. The Whitley, with a big, underslung jaw, flew nose down, tail up. The Heinkel 111 flew nose-up, looking like a well-fed shark (except that the rear half of its body didn't waggle as it went). The Junkers 88 had a distinctive motor-bus appearance, rugged and businesslike. The Spitfire was graceful, all perfect lines and curves – obviously 'right'. The Hurricane looked rugged but wrong – as a North country-man remarked: 'That's t'feller wi' 'oomped back and straight wings.' Their opponent, the Messerschmitt 109, was an angular job – apparently designed by a professor of geometry with a passion for straight lines; but his Me 110 seemed to have had a sailplane for ancestor.

Instant recognition in action could only be developed out of an intense interest in aeroplanes, frequent visits to aerodromes, and detailed study of hundreds of photographs. Merely to look at silhouettes and repeat after me 'The Dornier Do 17 is a high-wing monoplane with two rudders and two engines' was next nearest to useless, and could easily be dangerous.

It was dangerous, even in the R.A.F. On 3rd March, 1940, Spitfires flying over Kent intercepted a monoplane with two motors and a twin-tail; they shot it down and killed all aboard – unfortunately, it was a Hudson. With its fat, bulky fuselage it was really nothing like the Dornier, which had been aptly named the 'Flying Pencil', but the Spitfires shot 'by the book'. There was no short cut to aircraft recognition.

Exactly the same held good for ships. An R.A.F. pilot, in the early stages of the escape of the *Scharnhorst*, *Gneisnau* and *Prinz Eugen*, when an airborne-radar failure had allowed them to come out undetected, actually flew right over them as they dashed up-Channel. He reported them as destroyers, though it was possible, he thought, that one of them might have had a tripod mast. Mistaking two battle-cruisers and one heavy cruiser, escorted by a swarm of destroyers and E-boats, for a destroyer flotilla took some doing, it might be thought; but he did it.

The fact is that a distant ship has no scale. It is perfectly possible to mistake the *Queen Mary* for a tug, and vice versa, provided the silhouettes are not too dissimilar. Only if the observer is close enough to make out a standard fitting, such as a lifeboat, can he with any certainty work out the size of the ship that carries it. Not airmen merely, but professional sailors, have been led astray in this way.

In September 1942, while surfaced at night, U-156 sighted a passenger steamer approaching. Hartenstein, one of the U-boat 'Aces' was in command. He had a brief argument with his number one, who estimated 6,000 tons. Hartenstein thought it was a trifle larger, probably 7 or 8,000 tons. He fired numbers 1 and 3 tubes at it and waited for the estimated two minutes to pass. Nothing happened, the passenger ship kept steadily on. Two and a half minutes, and still no sign of a hit. Three minutes. The ship was lit up by the moon, a white wash under her bows, going serenely on her way. Hartenstein turned away, furious at his own sudden incompetence. Then there were two vivid flashes and the rumbling roar of the torpedoes striking the ship, and she started to call for help, giving her name.

The U-boat picked up the transmission and her officers thumbed rapidly through their Ship List. Ah. *Laconia*, Cunard

White Star, 19,695 tons. Nearly 20,000 tons! That explained the long wait – they had fired at what they thought was a small ship near to them and what in fact they were looking at was a large ship far away.

That mistake was made by naval officers; by men who were not under strain, had plenty of time, and were thoroughly and professionally used to ships. A pilot, attacking low down, might have only two or three seconds in which to identify the ship he was approaching and to drop his bombs. Small wonder there were mistakes. And small wonder, too, that ships were nervy.

From a distance, there was no difference between a 1,000 ton collier and a 10,000 ton tanker. The silhouettes were identical, the typical types of both classes having the engines at the stern, and usually the bridge as well. Sometimes, the bridge is amidships – on its own, looking rather lonely. Other, non-typical colliers, look like any other merchant ship except that a close inspection would reveal that the hatches were unusually large – to allow large crane grabs to plumb into them, for more rapid discharge. But even an expert, from a distance, could give you no idea of the size of the ship; and if he could, it would mean nothing until you had agreed on the terms of reference – whether gross tonnage, deadweight tonnage, displacement tonnage, net tonnage, or under-deck tonnage. A ship of 5,000 tons gross might have a deadweight tonnage of 9,000 tons; a liner of 20,000 gross tons a deadweight tonnage of only 4,000 tons. Aircrews' heads began to spin, when confronted with this awful chaos, quite apart from the difficulty of actual recognition.

And this again was complicated by the fact that the Germans had conquered Europe; some of the ships they had captured, and some of them had come over to us. A single ship, sailing unescorted, might be a German ocean-raider slipping through the Channel to the Atlantic – or it might be a straggler from a British convoy. Sometimes they straggled because they couldn't keep up; sometimes because they were fed up. When seen, they might be reported as anything. Four merchant ships in the Channel, one one occasion, were reported as a squadron of battleships! And in March 1943, the German blockade-runner *Doggerbank* (ex-British *Speybank*), returning from the Far East, escaped the vigilance of our naval and air patrols. But she did not escape the German Navy. U-43 sighted and sank her off the Canaries.

By far the best oddentification, however, took place in the Mediterranean in 1941. A tanker, British, met an aircraft, German. The German mistook the British for Italian, and the British mistook the German for British. The Messerschmitt fell in as escort for the tanker, and the tanker gratefully accepted the offer. Along came a British bomber – a Blenheim – and seeing a tanker escorted by a Messerschmitt assumed it to be Italian, and attacked it. The German fighter then sallied forth to defend the British tanker from the British bomber; and the tanker, seeing the Blenheim come in on a bombing run, thought it was German. They not only fired at it – they hit it. Under attack from a British ship and a German aircraft, the Blenheim near-missed, and fled. Then up came a complete R.A.F. squadron of Maryland bombers, and, seeing the Messerschmitt-defended tanker, dived in to finish it off. At the last moment, their leader spotted the Red Duster flying from the stern, and swerved. By that time, the Messerschmitt had gone home, glowing with the consciousness of duty done.

A more mysterious happening took place off the east coast, where a convoy was met at dawn, the usual time, by a Blenheim. From 6 o'clock until 7.45, the Blenheim circled protectively then put in an attack. The bombs were well-aimed, falling towards the centre of the convoy. Captain Hadlow, of the collier *Grangetoft*, actually saw the first bomb drop away from the Blenheim. It was an astonishing sight. What happened next was even more astounding. The bomb fell in the usual arc towards the ship steaming next ahead of him – and struck the wireless aerial; and the aerial, tightening like a tennis-net, slung the bomb back! It went up and out, clear of the ship.

It is hardly possible that a Blenheim pilot had made this mistake. It is just possible that the convoy had made a mistake – that what they had taken for a Blenheim was actually a Junkers 88. The types were not too dissimilar, and the German markings might have been removed for the purpose. There was a definite case of this, on 21st September, 1940. A Ju 88 shot down near Bosham, Sussex, into a field by the railway line, seemed to have counted on this similarity in silhouette. It was camouflaged in a neutral brown and green; there were no black crosses on it, no swastika, no markings of any sort except the squadron crest – a red lion on a white shield. On close inspection, it could be seen that the markings were in fact still there – painted over.

Or it might have been a captured Blenheim, taking advantage

of the fact that the R.A.F. dared not give night cover to convoys, but usually sent an escort for the two critical times of dawn and dusk. Normal German aircraft did try to pretend they were the escort, coming out to the convoy from over the land; and this in part explains why the ships were so trigger-happy.

Their gunners never did learn aircraft recognition, and the final admission of the fact was made in time for the Normandy landings. There would be about 11,000 Allied planes over the invasion beaches – and about 200 German. It would be disastrous if the ships blazed away indiscriminately, in their usual fashion. They could put up an astounding barrage, heavier than the London guns, heavier even than Scapa Flow.

The first action taken was to ignore the old national markings, which no one could see anyway, and to jazz-up every Allied aircraft taking part with gigantic black and white stripes on all under-wing surfaces, with blazing white, five-pointed stars elsewhere. The final stage was to gather a large number of men from the Observer Corps and embark them in the ships as a guide to the gunners. Mostly old men, too frail for any normal form of active service, they were a mine of extraordinary aeronautical lore. Not for them the Dorniers and Focke Wulfs – kid stuff, that, any young fool could tell one of those ten miles away – no, they really became excited only over the very latest, most obscure and exotic machines – some of them still a rumour. If any men could do the job, they could – if they weren't sea-sick.

They arrived, for the invasion, at the former H.Q. of the Channel Guard near Southampton, now a D.E.M.S. Depot, and were greeted by Commander Spencer. There were 350 of them, assembled as on parade before him, and he hardly knew how to address them. They were all in civilian clothes, with brassards; some were barristers, some were road-sweepers and some were Admirals (Retired). He began: '*Gentlemen*, you can do what you like while you are here – but you cannot smoke during working hours.' They found, surprisingly, that *H.M.S.* '*Safeguard*' did have one or two things to teach them; one of them said later that that period was his 'best fortnight of the war'.

When they went down to the ships, lying covering all the waters of Spithead and the Solent in a vast armada, to take over aircraft spotting, they were greeted by a 'Thank God for you, chum' from the gunners. And doubtless the airmen felt much happier, too. On the night of 5th/6th June, with a heavy sea running, they put out for Normandy. The wheel had come round, at last, full circle. What the Germans had threatened only, we would do.

14 · Normandy

On the night of 5th June, the German radar station on Cap de la Hogue, near Cherbourg, reported shipping echoes round the Isle of Wight. At the nightly Naval Conference, held in Paris just before midnight, the report was considered – and dismissed as just another convoy, perhaps the 'Coal-Scuttle Brigade' coming out from the Motherbank. At ten minutes to two, the officers were roused from their beds by a flurry of reports from all the radar stations. They were reporting widespread 'interference' – there were so many echoes on the screens that the operators could not believe that they were being caused by ships. But they were.

The Naval staff tried to get in touch with the radar stations by telephone and teleprinter – and found that the lines had been cut. The Maquis were at work. And at 3.30 that morning, 6th June, German Seventh Army H.Q. received via its forward units the ominous report: 'Parachutists.'

The leading assault craft were three hours away, rolling and plunging in the black night of a June gale, towards the beaches of Normandy. They did not come in a wave, or even in a succession of waves, they came in line ahead in lines that reached back to Spithead. As the first landing craft raced in to touch down on the coast of France, the ships were still pouring out of the great anchorage between Portsmouth and the Isle of Wight. There were five battleships there, and two monitors, and 19 cruisers and 77 destroyers; there were landing ships and landing craft, coasters and colliers, gunboats and tugs beyond count. A living bridge of ships between England and Normandy. They moved along the swept channels in the minefields like some vast conveyor-belt out of a madman's imagination – a conveyor-belt held in place by the destroyers and corvettes, their stained hulls rising to the raging swell, their angry guns raking the horizon with each rise and fall of the sea. It was the greatest seaborne invasion in the history of the world. And the minesweepers, patient ploughmen of the Channel, led it in.

Bomber Command had pulverised the gun positions, 1,000 American bombers had drenched the coastal areas. The villages, in that grey dawn along that holiday shore showed shattered roofs and black and empty windows like the eye-sockets of skulls. Smoke drifted away among the houses and spouts of spray leapt from the water as the landing craft came in. The shrill, uneven chatter of Spandaus greeted them from the dunes, from the headlands, from the holiday villages, like crazy xylophonists half-drowned by the continuous wailing, howling thunder of fire from the support craft. Soon, they were joined by the slower steady put-put-put of the Brens, where infantry came up to the beach and flopped among the dunes and behind the sea walls; and soon, that too was gone with the Spandaus as the battle moved inland.

Off Selsey Bill, tugs were raising the Phoenix caissons sunk there long ago in readiness. The great steel boxes were pumped out, rose slowly above the surface. From Langstone Harbour, from the Beaulieu river they were being raised and towed out. The 'Mulberries' were getting ready to go to Normandy. Doomed coasters and colliers, low laden in the water, moved slowly out to Normandy; sluggishly and slow, filled with concrete, they wallowed down the 'Spout' – the broad, swept channel in the minefields that pointed to the Bay of the Seine, and the left flank of the beachhead. They were 'Gooseberry' – to be sunk in a half circle, as breakwater against any sudden Channel gale. Within sound of the guns, they sank until only their upper works showed, a solid barrier to the sea.

And in every harbour of the south coast lay colliers and coasters, ready, practised and waiting. Colliers usually carry coal – usually, but not always; this time, they did not. On D+1 – 7th June – the *Jesmond* of Blyth, manned entirely by 'Geordies' except for her master, John Wilson, who was a Scot, stood out from Shoreham towards the narrow end of the 'Spout'. That point, soon to be known as 'Piccadilly Circus', was where the ships entered the funnel – at the broad mouth of it lay Normandy; and if you went in, that's where you came out. You could nearly walk it, from the Isle of Wight to Normandy, there were so many ships.

In her holds, which for four years had carried Northumberland and Durham coal to feed the lights of London, she held this day the men, the Bofors guns, the ammunition and stores of a Light Anti-Aircraft Regiment. These she was to spill out onto the shores of Normandy. They had practised embarking

114

and disembarking on an open beach for a month beforehand, and they had it taped. As she came down the 'Spout', the little collier – under 750 tons – was passed by ship after ship, larger and faster than she was. Two-thirds of them flew the 'Red Duster' of the British merchant navy, less than a third the Stars and Stripes. These were the waters where the British colliers had been savaged in 1940, and now the colliers were going back.

From all along the south coast, they converged upon the Nab. From the west and from the east they sailed, from under Dunnose cliff and past Selsey, to meet in the waters where Convoy C.W.9, four years ago, had been blindly harried to destruction by the E-boats and the Stukas. There, they converged, and there they turned, hundreds of them – turning their bows for France.

To seaward of the 'Spout', and on both sides, the M.T.B.s of Coastal Forces reared and plunged in the Channel waves, watching for the E-boats that never came; and the minesweepers busily swept and re-swept the channel and enlarged it. As the coasters steamed on, there was a shaking in the air. At first, no sound at all, hardly more than a distant vibration; and then nearer, clearer, and unmistakable – the sound of the guns in France, as the battle rolled forward through the bloody bocage. It was made up, too, of the cracking broadsides of the battleships and cruisers, as they stood off the beachhead and hurtled their shells miles inland, onto some dusty Norman village, into some lazy orchard, at some distant cross-roads and left a plunging chaos of screaming horses, suddenly disembowelled, and burning, blazing Wehrmacht trucks. The *Courbet* was there, her 12-inch guns pointed at her own country, firing on the land from which she had fled in June 1940. For now, it was June 1944. Now, it was our turn.

Overhead the bombers flew. When they came, they stretched for two hundred miles, formation after formation, so that while the leaders were turning for home, with the great bomb carpets spurting up and shrouding the rolling Norman countryside, the last formations were still over England, flying out to the Channel, the faint stutter of machine-gun fire drifting down from them, as they tested their guns.

The coast of France was a thin grey line, on a grey day. Hard to believe, but there it was – at last. Woods and hills could be made out, and two church spires standing close together in a cluster of houses; and ships lying off the beaches. Ships that no one could count. They lay along the coast for twenty miles, they poured down the 'Spout' to Normandy, more of them, and still more. Of merchant ships alone, there were 6,488. The 'Red Duster' rode, virtually unopposed, upon the waters.

Red wreck flags stuck out of the water, close inshore. There were landing craft down there, and men, moved by the tides as the tides moved. There was oil upon the water – oil fuel – and wreckage. Compo boxes floated past and bits of aeroplanes, and dead, drowned men. A parachute unfolded over the beach-head; watched by thousands, it drifted down – to collapse in a field of corn, beaten flat, behind the beach defences. The emplacements still stared out to sea, unbroken by the bombardment, but smothered and stunned by it, so that in most places – though not all – the assault troops had gone over them with a rush. Not all. On those headlands and in those dusty fields torn to ribbons by the tracks of tanks and wheels of vehicles there were rifles. Mounds of earth, with rifles driven muzzle-first into the soil at their head, and a helmet slung carelessly on them and jingling in the wind, British, Canadian, American, German – and little tins and jam jars with pathetic bunches of wayside flowers, too, placed there by children.

The Mulberry jetties were being placed in position – tugs in a continuous stream were towing them over from England. Each one would form a harbour as large as Dover. Off the shore, miles out, the warships stood, and hammered the morning. Closer in lay the big Liberty ships, bulky and arrogant, that had easily caught up and passed the coasters on the run across. But now it was the coasters' turn.

From the big ships a swarm of lesser craft ferried ashore to the beaches their packed cargoes of men and guns and vehicles. The colliers and the other coasters did not wait for that.

The *Jesmond* drove straight for the beach. She was a coastal collier, built to operate in shallow water. As she came in to Normandy she slowed, and slowly grounded, below the high-tide mark. For four weeks she had practised; daily the soldiers had got their guns ashore in conditions just like this, near Shoreham. In minutes, they were ashore, and the Bofors went bouncing up the beach, past the staring eyes of an undamaged gun emplacement, part of the West Wall, into a gap in the dunes, and out of sight; the men a little tense, excited, standing a little straighter, with that tight feeling at the back of the neck that you get when you know there's an enemy ahead, and you're going to meet him. They were gone, to be swallowed up some-

116

where in the bocage, in the battle for Tilly or Carpiquet or Falaise.

The sailors waited for the tide; then full-speed astern and they drew off – and back to England for more. They loaded more Bofors guns, more men – R.A.F. Regiment this time – and set course for the 'Spout'.

Within an hour of leaving the coast two fighters ripped down on them, machine-guns and canon blazing at the collier. The Mate, George Atkinson, went down with a bullet in the leg; thirteen of the R.A.F. men were hit. With rough and ready methods, they probed for the bullet in the Mate's leg, found it, removed it, and bound up the wound. He carried on, limping, and the *Jesmond* carried on to Normandy.

In the first fortnight after the invasion she went four times to Normandy, carrying men and guns and equipment. But, while the little coastal colliers were ferrying to France, much bigger colliers had now entered the Channel. 6,000 tonners were now operating. The conveyor-belt of ships between France and England was anchored to Spithead and the Solent. Many of those ships were coal-burners, and they had continually to be re-bunkered. Large stocks of fuel had already been brought through the Channel and stored in the Portsmouth area, and these had to be kept up; supplies had also to be taken out to the ships lying at anchor off the northern shores of the Isle of Wight. There were thousands of them, so many that it was impossible for them to come into harbour to fuel. They had to be bunkered where they were, and a fleet of small craft took out to them their coal, their oil, and their provisions. They lay from Spithead in the east right round to the Needles in the west – a forest of masts.

As a matter of sheer organisation, it was fantastic. Everything was pressed into service. There were big colliers like the *Kingsborough* and the *Kingsland*, bringing in huge supplies of bulk fuel; there was even the *Chemong*, under Captain Landreth – an ex-Lake Huron steamer, built in Montreal. And there were little dredgers, like the *Lypta I*, which used their cranes to shift coal into the invasion fleet instead of collecting sand for air raid shelters or mud dumping. Every big ship had a swarm of little ships, supplying her wants on the spot, like flies round the honey. In no other way could the conveyor-belt be kept turning endlessly. Even the tugs, busy off Sesley, raising and then towing over to France the hundreds of sections of 'Mulberry', had their essential needs like any larger ship, they had

117

to be supplied with oil fuel and water and provisions.

When 70 merchant ships appeared in the Straits on 9th September, 1940, steaming on the German side of the Channel, and moving from Boulogne towards Calais, people in Dover thought the invasion was imminent, that the menacing sight portended the landing of field-grey troops that night or the next night. Those 70 ships could have anchored at Spithead, any time in the summer of 1944, and no one would have noticed that they were there.

That armada, largely a British armada, carried to Normandy in the first fourteen days after the landings 638,045 soldiers, 97,668 vehicles, 224,636 tons of materials and supplies. And the scenes at Spithead and in the Solent were precisely half the problem. They had not only to load, they had to unload – across open beaches, with no harbours at all, except those we had ourselves constructed and towed across. The coasters went straight in to the beaches – at least those did that were captained by skilful and determined masters, as most of them were – but the big ships had to lie off. From them the specially-designed landing craft – from tiny assault craft to cumbrous 'Rhino' rafts – ferried guns and vehicles, workshops and stores, millions of different items, so that the fields of Normandy were one vast ordnance park and it was difficult to find any room there at all.

The German blitzkrieg of 1940, brilliant though it undoubtedly was, had never confronted its planners with any such problems as these. And the truth of the German invasion plans of 1940 is that, flushed with triumph, they thought they could throw a force across the Channel, until slowly it was borne in upon them that they did not possess even so much as one of the essential requirements. They were a land-animal trying to get across the seas at a sea-animal, and they had no luck. It was not to be expected.

It was the sea, far more than the Germans, which threatened the Normandy landings; and again, that was to be expected, for the sea was the real problem. Forts can be cracked open by high explosive, grimly determined defenders can be shocked and stunned into temporary ineffectiveness as the defenders of the West Wall largely were stunned; but the sea is a different matter. On D+13 it rose and hurled itself against the beaches, it smashed against the ships and landing craft, it drove them from their anchors and hurled them stranded on the shore. It broke in a white, foaming fury on the sunken, cement-laden coasters of 'Gooseberry' – but they held. It smashed at 'Mulberry B', the

British-built, British-erected artificial harbour – and it held. It smashed at 'Mulberry A', British-built too, but American-erected, carelessly, in a hurry, badly maintained*—and 'Mulberry A' was smashed to fragments and thrown up on the shore, to lie there to this day. Mines broke loose and, floating through the storm-tossed seas, among plunging ships, sank some of them. The gale was so tremendous that convoys off the English coasts were driven back to port. On the shores of Normandy 800 ships and landing craft were stranded. Only the slow, methodical work put into the erection of the British 'Mulberry' and the protection given by the sunken colliers of the 'Gooseberries' prevented an utter disaster and the driving of our forces into the sea.

But they did hold, and we recovered, and the build-up went on. More Divisions, armoured and infantry, were coming – and a Channel convoy, in July 1944, was a mightily different matter to the hard-fought passage of the little colliers four years before.

The convoy which cleared Southend on Sunday, 30th July, 1944, differed also in one minor respect from the ill-fated C.W.8 which had sailed to its destruction in the Straits of Dover on 'Black Thursday', 25th July, 1940. It contained passengers, and they had nothing to do except eat, sleep and enjoy the sunshine and sea air. Their tanks and trucks and half-tracks were stowed in the holds, and for four days they were on holiday. Some sat on deck and read a book, others washed their dog, and one kept a diary. He had so much time, he could keep it minute by minute.

In July 1940, it was forbidden for any man of the Royal Navy or the Merchant Service to keep a diary. It was probably forbidden in 1944, but no one cared. The warships logged incidents as they occurred, for no one can accurately remember a rapid sequence of such events even an hour or two later, and from those logs the action reports were made out on which the official histories would later be based. But these reports were necessarily spare and bleak, the framework of the battle, but not the feeling of it or the sight and sound and smell of it. For the most part, all that survives of the Channel Battles of 1940 is the memory of them, recalled 17 years afterwards. And yet these prove surprisingly accurate, when checked against such meagre records as have been published. The merchant navy gunner who

---

* Chester Wilmot, *The Struggle For Europe*, p. 322, and anyone who saw it.

sailed with C.W.8 remembered the ambulance planes which dogged them and recalled that he saw one which had been shot down, lying wrecked at Dover. A photograph, published at the time in the aeronatucial press, shows this aircraft floating under the harbour wall with most of its wings missing. What men remembered, they remembered with considerable accuracy; but memory is selective, some things must have been forgotten and will remain therefore forever lost.

All Saturday the convoy, the largest since D-Day, was forming up off Southend; the big, packed troopships moving slowly down river from Tilbury. They had sailed very early in the morning or late the previous night. They were carrying the 1st Polish Armoured Division to their rendezvous with death.* The Poles knew they were going to die – it could be heard in their singing, in their tones, in their conversation, seen in their attitude and in their faces, and in the way they held themselves. They were trying to return to their own country, with the German Army barring the way and the Red Army already letting Warsaw die, and they knew it was a dream. They formed choirs and sang, beautifully, hauntingly. They sang 'Tipperary', and it sounded sad and beautiful.

As they came down river in the night, singing, the doodle-bugs came speeding across the sunset with yellow flame at their tails, like comets. There was a stream of them, fleeting across the docks; as each one fell, spluttering to silence, the yellow glow sank slowly towards the darkening rooftops of London, then slanted down with an increasing steepness. It moved remorselessly down towards the houses where families sat at supper and lovers held hands in the cinemas. It touched them – and there was an ugly orange-red glow that spread for an agonising two or three seconds; then a slow, curling column of smoke and brick dust billowing upwards.

Shortly, the moonlight cut a path upon the water and shone in the silver fire along the gun barrels of the ships, upon the high gun-platforms that studded their decks like toadstools. And then, when the blind robots fell into the great city, the masts and derricks of all the ships were lit blood-red.

At dawn, they pass through the outer balloon line, guarding London, and hear the sirens wailing from the shore. Ships

* It was a statistic certainty, as far as front-line troops were concerned, that almost all would be killed or wounded within six months. Some units were reduced to half strength in a month or two.

jostle and pass each other. A Yankee tank landing craft comes up the Thames, with three bold swastikas daubed on the bridge, and men cheer across the water; another Polish troopship passes them, crammed with men and vehicles and guns – and the cheering echoes and re-echoes between the ships.

By tea-time, there were forty 8,000-ton transports lying at anchor off Southend, and in the haze, beyond counting, a maze of big landing ships, frigates, and balloon ships. They lay there all that day, in the sunshine, with the angry guns sprinkling the sky with black shell-bursts, like currants, and Kent a sunlit patchwork of woods and wheat going down to a sea of blue and green. It was golden weather, as the great convoy lay poised between the Battle of London and the Battle of France.

All that night, too, they lay there, crammed to the last inch with tanks and guns and men; the British among them joked about the *Altmark*, so close-packed were the hammocks, so small the chance of ever reaching the gangway if anything should happen. There were so many men in that doomed Division they had taken a day to pass through London, the great convoys roaring endless through the capital – the tanks, the half-tracks, the command vehicles, the trucks, the guns, with the men sitting in them feeling themselves already off to some gigantic rodeo, with web equipment across their shoulders and cartridge pouches at their belts, and inn-keepers standing free drinks to the few British soldiers they saw.

On Sunday, 30th July, smoke began to roll up from the convoy. The Captains were coming back from the Commodore's conference. The dull roar of depth charges rolled in from the open sea – a few U-boats were operating in the Channel, now that they had the Schnorkel which made them less vulnerable in shallow water; now that the targets were no longer small colliers but ships well worth the risk, and now that the fate of the world depended on stopping them. Between July and December, 1944, they sank 60 ships around the coast, in the Channel, and off the invasion beaches.

At two o'clock precisely, the signal flying from the Commodore's ship became executive; that is, it came fluttering down – meaning: 'Proceed'. And then, precisely, one after the other – and not in a gaggle – the Liberty ships hauled up their anchors, and steamed in single file through the 'Gate' in the boom. There, the masts of a sunken ship pointed skew-wiff out of the water, drunkenly slanted. To port and starboard the mass of the convoy lay, waiting their turn to go out; ahead, an attenuated

¹ine of ships stretched as far as eye could see, their hulls showing above the horizon and black funnel smoke rolling across the endless water. A butterfly flew across the bows of one of the transports, the last trace of England.

To port and starboard the calm sea stretched blue and green, holding in its surface silver and pink reflections of the afternoon clouds; astern it was burnished and brilliant, and the black and shiny bodies of porpoises broke that silver surface, as they played. The gunners were uncovering the Oerlikons now; as the jagged hull of a wreck went by to starboard, they began to test the guns, the cannon shells screaming out over the water in pink points of fire. A wrecked ship went by to port; and there were the leaping water spouts and thunder boom of the escort testing heavier armament. From here and there in the convoy, smoke-screens went billowing away, as ships tested the canisters; the single mast of another sunken wreck went past to port, and two Spitfires circled the convoy like high-flying gulls. They were close escort, and that meant: 'Special convoy'.

Mile upon mile stretched the lines of ships, against a red-tinged sky, in which floated great cumulus clouds, like icebergs, casting their image in the sea. As the convoy rounded the North Foreland for the run into the Channel, the colour of the sea changed to a cold blue; an escorting corvette passed down the lines of ships, her crew waving up to the soldiers lining the rails. The leading warship turned still more to starboard, hull and upperworks hardly visible now in the sunset haze, the winking signals flashing from her bridge. A great half-circle of ships came turning into the Straits, with an Air-Sea Rescue launch passing through their ranks, homeward bound.

As the moon came out over the sea there was the dull thumping sound of explosions from the rear of the convoy, and a momentary spurt of tracers, far away. A half-hearted air attack. From the leading ships, it was hardly visible.

Above Dover a single searchlight swept the sky and the white cliffs were faintly visible; to port the Pas de Calais was shrouded in moonhaze. The black shapes of the convoy, huddled closer for protection against E-boats, seemed to strain forward, as if to clear the Straits in a bound. Many bore on hull and bridge the scars of shelling from the cross-Channel guns. No shells came, the only sound was the melancholy message of the bell-buoys; yet it was as if each squat, slow-riding ship was leaning forward, like a horse about to clear an obstacle. Every soldier was under orders to stay below decks, but one or two were lurking in the shadow of the ventilators, in order to savour the moment. As midnight passed and nothing happened, they went below.

In the morning, out of the mist which shrouded them at dawn, out to sea on the port side, comes the grumble and thump of depth-charging where a single U-boat tries to attack the convoy. This mist begins to close in on the ships; then they begin to turn, turning for France, with the sun like a pale moon above the mast, the ships huddling together, dropping fog-floats; finally, each ship is alone, hemmed in by the haze.

Bombers are passing above, all the time, the brrrp brrrp as they test their guns striking down to the Channel. An LCT suddenly appears under the bow of one of the ships, they are racing towards each other; and behind the first LCT, four more. The LCTs veer into the middle of the convoy and go down between the lines, heading for England. As the mist clears slightly, the leading frigate is visible. She is turning away to starboard, and the flashes from her lamp are winking fast at the convoy, which turns behind her. The cause – five minsweepers, with floats out, and flying red flags – loom up and shave past the convoy to port.

Rapidly, the mist is clearing. There is a complete convoy approaching, and passing down the port side – all Liberty ships; then a host of smaller vessels, then bunches of LCTs – more than thrity in the first lot. This is the conveyor-belt in operation – rather like rush-hour in Regent Street.

And then, the convoy begins to lose speed, the engines slowing down – and quite clearly now, to port, the sound of the guns.

They were going down the side of the Liberty ship, down rope ladders, hand-over-hand, in full marching order, with rifles slung over their shoulders. Below an LCT rolled alongside, the gap between it and the transport opening and narrowing with the push and tug of the sea. It was fifty feet below them, and this was no time to slip. Above them, the ship's loudhailer was blaring out a military march.

Then the trucks came swaying out of the hold of the transport, they swung outboard and hovered over the rolling LCT. As they came down towards her deck, the soldiers grabbed the swinging wheels of the three-ton vehicles and manoeuvred them into position on the floor of the LCT. Then the LCT drew away and anchored in the lee of 'Gooseberry', the soldiers taking no notice of the sunken colliers, there was so much to see. 'What's this place, chum?' they asked a young rating. 'Juno Beach, but you won't be going in a while yet.' Another LCT came alongside them, with half-a-dozen Polish tanks and a couple of soft-skinned vehicles aboard.

One Englishman jumped the distance, and was soon sitting in the turret of a tank, headphones on, listening to the news from London; two others had gone over the side for a swim. When the tide was right, the LCT started up at a quiet order from the Lieutenant commanding it, and headed in for the beach. The soldiers got into their lorries and tanks, the drivers started their engines. As the LCT hit the beach, there was another quiet order from the Lieutenant and two ratings, stationed forward, in three seconds lowered the bows flat on the sand to form a ramp. The trucks and tanks instantly drove forward, whined and groaned up the beach, spurting sand from wheels and tracks, and were gone amongst the dunes. When they thought about it all, later, they saw why the Germans failed in 1940 to invade at all, and if they had, would have met irretrievable disaster.

On 6th September, the V.1 bombardment of London docks ceased. The Canadians had over-run the launching sites. The German coastal batteries furiously re-doubled their fire, for they knew their hour was near. There was no point now in conserving ammunition or worrying about barrel wear.

17th September was a clear, sunny day. Third Canadian Division was spread out before Boulogne. They could actually see England, as a faint, white line on the horizon. These were the men who had bought off collier seamen splinters of shells fired by the Calais-Boulogne batteries. Now, they were going to see the batteries close up and interview the gunners personally. With them were the curious tracked vehicles of the 79th Armoured Division (the 'Funnies'). The R.A.F. struck the first blow, with 690 bombers, and took all morning to do it, bombing from a height at target indicators planted by the Pathfinders.

The high ground where the batteries were completely vanished from sight in billowing clouds of brown and black smoke. It was, said a Canadian officer, 'an awesome sight; it was hard to believe that any enemy troops could remain alive in the target areas.'

As the infantry, with the diamond shoulder flashes of '3 Div', rose up and went forward, Spandaus began to chatter at them, and men pitched forward; then came the shellfire, heavy and accurate. The attack slowed, and there was bitter, stubborn fighting. The Germans had suffered few casualties and their fortified positions had been virtually undamaged by the bombs. The Dover batteries had done better. They had engaged the Calais guns, to prevent them joining in the battle – and they had hit and knocked out a German 16-inch gun at a range of 42,000 yards. In addition, they scored repeated hits within the battery positions.

There were four British guns taking part in this action – two 14-inchers of the Royal Marine Siege Regiment plus 'Jane' and 'Clem', two 15-inchers manned by 540 Coast Regiment, R.A. It was a brilliant performance.

The old Citadel, which had shrugged off an enormous tonnage of bombs, fell – in the best traditions of historical romance – by a French civilian claiming to know of a 'secret tunnel' leading into the heart of the fortifications. A single platoon of the Stormont, Dundas and Glengarry Highlanders followed him into the tunnel – and came out in the middle of the fort, behind the German's backs. Simultaneously, two 'Funnies' blew in the gate. That was too much for the defenders and 'a host of white flags waved from the walls'.*

Calais was next. The 7th Brigade went for the town; the 8th Brigade for the batteries between Sangatte and Cap Blanc Nez. Again, there was the same preliminary air and gun bombardment, which served to quieten the opposition a little, psychologically at any rate. By the 26th all Germans in the battery positions were dead or taken.

Last to fall was Cap Gris Nez, twelve miles from Calais and the nearest part of the continent to England. The guns and Kesselring's old command post fell to the 9th Brigade on 29th September, with 1,600 prisoners. The forty-nine months bombardment of the Straits was over.

The Channel was free again.

* Eye-witness, quoted in *The Canadian Army 1939–45*.

THE RED BERET

by
Hilary St. George Saunders

This is the story of Arnhem, Bruneval, the Ardennes, Normandy, the crossing of the Rhine. It is the story of the Red Devils, the most heroic band of daredevils any war has ever produced.

NEW ENGLISH LIBRARY   40p

NEL BESTSELLERS

Crime

T013 332	CLOUDS OF WITNESS	Dorothy L. Sayers 40p
T016 307	THE UNPLEASANTNESS AT THE BELLONA CLUB	Dorothy L. Sayers 40p
W003 011	GAUDY NIGHT	Dorothy L. Sayers 40p
T010 457	THE NINE TAILORS	Dorothy L. Sayers 35p
T012 484	FIVE RED HERRINGS	Dorothy L. Sayers 40p
T015 556	MURDER MUST ADVERTISE	Dorothy L. Sayers 40p

Fiction

W002 775	HATTER'S CASTLE	A. J. Cronin 60p
T013 944	CRUSADER'S TOMB	A. J. Cronin 60p
T013 936	THE JUDAS TREE	A. J. Cronin 50p
T001 288	THE TROUBLE WITH LAZY ETHEL	Ernest K. Gann 30p
T003 922	IN THE COMPANY OF EAGLES	Ernest K. Gann 30p
W002 145	THE NINTH DIRECTIVE	Adam Hall 25p
T012 271	THE WARSAW DOCUMENT	Adam Hall 40p
T012 778	QUEEN IN DANGER	Adam Hall 30p
T007 243	SYLVIA SCARLETT	Compton Mackenzie 30p
T007 669	SYLVIA AND ARTHUR	Compton Mackenzie 30p
T007 677	SYLVIA AND MICHAEL	Compton Mackenzie 35p
T009 084	SIR, YOU BASTARD	G. F. Newman 30p
T009 769	THE HARRAD EXPERIMENT	Robert H. Rimmer 40p
T010 252	THE REBELLION OF YALE MARRATT	Robert H. Rimmer 40p
T013 820	THE DREAM MERCHANTS	Harold Robbins 75p
T012 255	THE CARPETBAGGERS	Harold Robbins 80p
T016 560	WHERE LOVE HAS GONE	Harold Robbins 75p
T013 707	THE ADVENTURERS	Harold Robbins 80p
T006 743	THE INHERITORS	Harold Robbins 60p
T009 467	STILETTO	Harold Robbins 30p
T015 289	NEVER LEAVE ME	Harold Robbins 40p
T016 579	NEVER LOVE A STRANGER	Harold Robbins 75p
T011 798	A STONE FOR DANNY FISHER	Harold Robbins 60p
T015 874	79 PARK AVENUE	Harold Robbins 60p
T011 461	THE BETSY	Harold Robbins 75p
T010 201	RICH MAN, POOR MAN	Irwin Shaw 80p
W002 186	THE PLOT	Irving Wallace 75p
T009 718	THE THREE SIRENS	Irving Wallace 75p
T010 341	THE PRIZE	Irving Wallace 80p

Historical

T009 750	THE WARWICK HEIRESS	Margaret Abbey 30p
T013 731	KNIGHT WITH ARMOUR	Alfred Duggan 40p
T013 758	THE LADY FOR RANSOM	Alfred Duggan 40p
T011 585	THE ROSE IN SPRING	Eleanor Fairburn 30p
T009 734	RICHMOND AND ELIZABETH	Brenda Honeyman 30p
T011 593	HARRY THE KING	Brenda Honeyman 35p
T009 742	THE ROSE BOTH RED AND WHITE	Betty King 30p
T010 988	BRIDE OF LIBERTY	Frank Yerby 30p
T014 649	FAIROAKS	Frank Yerby 50p
T014 045	TREASURE OF PLEASANT VALLEY	Frank Yerby 35p

Science Fiction

T011 410	EARTHWORKS	Brian Aldiss 25p
T014 576	THE INTERPRETER	Brian Aldiss 30p
T014 347	SPACE RANGER	Isaac Asimov 30 p
T016 900	STRANGER IN A STRANGE LAND	Robert Heinlein 75 p
W002 908	STAR BEAST	Robert Heinlein 30 p
T011 534	I WILL FEAR NO EVIL	Robert Heinlein 75 p
W002 684	THE HEAVEN MAKERS	Frank Herbert 30 p
T011 844	DUNE	Frank Herbert 75 p